W9-BUJ-676

WITHDRAWN
LVC BISHOP LIBRARY

THE SECRET GARDEN

Nature's Magic

LEBANON VALLEY COLLEGE LIBRARY

TWAYNE'S MASTERWORK STUDIES

Robert Lecker, General Editor

THE SECRET GARDEN

Nature's Magic

Phyllis Bixler

TWAYNE PUBLISHERS
An Imprint of Simon & Schuster Macmillan
New York

PRENTICE HALL INTERNATIONAL
London Mexico City New Delhi Singapore Sydney Toronto

Twayne's Masterwork Studies No. 161

The Secret Garden: Nature's Magic
Phyllis Bixler

Copyright © 1996 by Twayne Publishers
All rights reserved. No part of this book may be reproduced or transmitted in any form
or by any means, electronic or mechanical, including photocopying, recording, or by
any information storage and retrieval system, without permission in writing from the
Publisher.

Twayne Publishers
An Imprint of Simon & Schuster Macmillan
1633 Broadway
New York, NY 10019

Library of Congress Cataloging-in-Publication Data

Bixler, Phyllis
  The secret garden : nature's magic / Phyllis Bixler.
      p. cm.—(Twayne's masterwork studies ; no. 161)
  Includes bibliographical references (p.) and index.
  ISBN 0-8057-8814-X (cloth). —ISBN 0-8057-8815-8 (paper)
  1. Burnett, Frances Hodgson, 1849–1924.   Secret garden.
2. Children's stories, American—History and criticism.   3. Gardens
in literature.   4. Nature in literature.   I. Title.   II. Series.
PS1214.S43B59   1996
813'.4—dc20   96-20031
                                                                           CIP

The paper used in this publication meets the minimum requirements of American
National Standard for Information Sciences—Permanence of Paper for Printed Library
Materials. ANSI Z39.48-1984. ∞ ™

10 9 8 7 6 5 4 3 2 1 (hc)
10 9 8 7 6 5 4 3 2 1 (pb)

Printed in the United States of America.

Contents

Note on the References and Acknowledgments   *vii*

Chronology: Frances Hodgson Burnett's Life and Works   *ix*

LITERARY AND HISTORICAL CONTEXT
1. *The Secret Garden* and the Golden Age
   of Children's Literature   3
2. *The Secret Garden* as a Classic   9
3. Critical Reception   13

A READING
4. "Mistress Mary, Quite Contrary" (Chapters 1–8)   25
5. "Might I Have a Bit of Earth?" (Chapters 9–12)   37
6. "I Am Colin" (Chapters 13–20)   43
7. Nest Building (Chapters 13–20)   52
8. Parental Reunions (Chapters 21–27)   62
9. Class and Gender   75

Approaches to Teaching   87

Notes and References   94

Selected Bibliography   99

Index   105

Frances Hodgson Burnett.

Reproduced by permission of the Henry E. Huntington Library and Art Gallery, San Marino, California.

Note on the References and Acknowledgments

All page numbers in parenthetical references are from Frances Hodgson Burnett, *The Secret Garden,* ed. Dennis Butts (Oxford and New York: Oxford University Press, 1987). For readers using other editions, page numbers are preceded by chapter numbers.

I thank the many scholars, students, and other Burnett lovers who have prodded me to grow as a reader of *The Secret Garden.* My personal response to the book I owe to my parents' nurturant love.

Chronology:
Frances Hodgson Burnett's Life and Works

1849   Frances Hodgson is born 24 November in Manchester, England. Her parents, Edwin Hodgson and Eliza Boond, married in 1844, already have two sons; two daughters will be born after Frances. The family enjoys a comfortable life in the suburbs, supported by Hodgson's business selling household furnishings.

1853   Frances's father dies; her mother, still pregnant with their last child, decides to run the business herself.

1854   The family temporarily lives with relatives, where five-year-old Frances enjoys a garden that, in her 1893 memoir, *The One I Knew the Best of All,* she will call an "enchanted" "Garden of Eden." Her recollection of this garden will contribute to the magic aura of the garden in *The Secret Garden* (1911). Frances's appetite for stories, especially fairy stories, is fed by Frances Browne's *Granny's Wonderful Chair* (1856), received as a reward for good behavior. Her desire to please others is encouraged by religious and moral tales about exemplary children. She will later borrow features from both fairy tales and exempla in writing stories for children.

1855   Economic distress moves the family into an iron-gated square of once-imposing houses now surrounded by the overcrowded lodgings of mill workers employed in the smut-spewing factories nearby—urban conditions described and deplored by Friedrich Engels, who also lives in Manchester. Always admonished to speak and act like a "lady," Frances is forbidden to play with the mill workers' children, but she surreptitiously uses their dialect much as Mary and Colin learn Dickon's

Yorkshire in *The Secret Garden;* Frances's fascination with dialect and interest in working-class life will be reflected also in some of her adult fiction set in both England and America, such as *That Lass o' Lowrie's* (1877) and *In Connection with the De Willoughby Claim* (1899). Frances and her siblings attend a Select Seminary for Young Ladies and Gentleman taught by three young women in their home. Frances entertains her school friends by orally composing stories, borrowing heavily from formula fiction in popular magazines; her mother and teachers encourage her writing of poetry and stories. Frances finds her way into an abandoned, walled garden and imagines a carpet of flowers replacing its refuse and weeds; this experience anticipates Mary's discovery of the locked garden in *The Secret Garden.*

1864	Manchester's economy plummets, in part because the American Civil War has interfered with the shipments of cotton needed in British textile mills. Frances's mother sells the business, and her brother invites them to join him in Tennessee.
1865	On 11 May, about a month after Confederate General Lee surrenders and President Lincoln is assassinated, the Hodgson family sails from Liverpool. The family arrives in war-ravaged Tennessee and moves into an abandoned log cabin in rural New Market, where they sometimes rely on the kindness of neighbors to fend off hunger. Frances, almost 16, befriends Swan Burnett, son of the local doctor.
1866	Frances's family moves to an even more isolated house, closer to Knoxville; here a mountain thicket she calls her "Bower" provides solitude and stirs her imagination.
1868	Several months before her nineteenth birthday, Frances publishes in *Godey's Lady's Book* two stories written to make money needed by her family; she is soon publishing fiction regularly in popular and more prestigious journals.
1872–1873	Frances spends 15 months in England, sending stories back to America for publication. She returns 19 September 1873 to marry Swan Burnett, now a physician; they settle in Knoxville.
1874	Son Lionel is born 20 September in Tennessee.
1876	Son Vivian is born 5 April in Paris, where Frances's stories support the family while Swan studies ophthalmology.
1877	The Burnetts move to Washington, D.C., where Swan establishes a medical practice. *That Lass o' Lowrie's* is the first of a

number of adult novels that sell well in both England and America and are praised by critics; Burnett adapts some of her fiction for the stage.

1879   Burnett meets Louisa May Alcott and Mary Mapes Dodge; she publishes the first of many stories in Dodge's *St. Nicholas Magazine* for children; some originate in tales she composed orally for her young sons.

1880   "Editha's Burglar," appearing in *St. Nicholas Magazine,* portrays an idealized child who has a beneficent effect on adults, much like the exemplary children in the moral tales Burnett had read as a child.

1881   *A Fair Barbarian* is the first of Burnett's several popular adult romances—*The Shuttle* (1907) and *T. Tembarom* (1913) are others—that, like the novels of Henry James, portray the adventures of Americans in Europe. As famous author and respected physician, the Burnetts enjoy a prominent place in Washington, D.C., society.

1883   Burnett's autobiographically based *Through One Administration* documents intrigue in the nation's capital and reflects increasing strains within her marriage. Untypical in her fiction, this realist novel has an unhappy ending; being compared favorably to works by Henry Adams, William Dean Howells, and Henry James, it marks the zenith of critical approval Burnett will achieve during her lifetime.

1884   Emotionally ill and unable to write, is treated by a mind healer in Boston, where Mary Baker Eddy has just helped establish the first Church of Christ Scientist. Burnett will never become a Christian Scientist, but she accepts some of its tenets, which will be reflected in the healing role attributed to mental attitude and natural medicine in *The Secret Garden.*

1886   *Little Lord Fauntleroy* depicts an American boy who inherits a British title and estate and wins the heart of his haughty grandfather. Though inspired by the personality of Burnett's younger son, Vivian, its protagonist also resembles the child paragons in moral tales, and his story, like many of the author's earlier love stories for adults, is an adaptation of the Cinderella tale. An immediate best-seller in English, it is soon translated into more than a dozen languages and spawns a variety of products such as Fauntleroy toys, playing cards, chocolates, and velvet suits with lace collars, as worn by its hero in Reginald Birch's illustrations for the book. The phenomenal success of *Little Lord Fauntleroy* makes Burnett a wealthy

	celebrity and encourages her to steer away from critically appreciated realist novels for adults toward popular romances for children and adults.
1887	"Sara Crewe" appears in *St. Nicholas Magazine;* it will later be adapted as a play (1903) and enlarged as a book (1905), both retitled *A Little Princess.* Burnett attends Queen Victoria's Jubilee in London; her fascination with royalty is reflected in Sara Crewe's desire to act like a princess, as well as in *The Lost Prince* (1915), her last book for children. For the next 25 years she maintains residences in England and sometimes in Italy as well as in the United States, crossing the Atlantic 33 times during her lifetime.
1888	*The Real Little Lord Fauntleroy,* Burnett's stage adaptation of her novel written to counter a pirated play by another author, opens in London and New York; a four-year Broadway run is followed by years of success on the road. Critics wonder when Burnett will fulfill the promise as an adult novelist earlier shown in *Through One Administration* (1883).
1890	*Little Saint Elizabeth and Other Stories* collects some of her fiction for children. *Nixie,* a play based on "Editha's Burglar" (1880), opens in London, establishing a decade of theatrical collaboration and close friendship with physician and actor Stephen Townesend. Townesend also helps Burnett care for her consumptive son Lionel, whose death at age 16 pivots Burnett into a long mourning that will be reflected in *Giovanni and the Other Children Who Have Made Stories* (1892). Partly in Lionel's memory, she increases her charitable works for sick and poor children in London. Undoubtedly, her experience with her invalid son and in children's hospitals provides insights later used in her portrayal of sickly Mary and Colin in *The Secret Garden.*
1893	In *The One I Knew the Best of All,* a memoir ending with the selling of her first story while still a teenager, Burnett emphasizes the childhood talents and experiences that led to her becoming an author.
1895	Swan moves out of the Burnetts' Washington, D.C., home; Frances's sister Edith and her husband move in; from now on Edith is often with Frances in Europe and America.
1896	Critics deplore the strong-willed heroine of *A Lady of Quality,* set in eighteenth-century England, but the romance sells well, and Burnett adapts it for the stage. Her adult fiction will continue to please a large audience, but she no longer receives

serious attention from the critics. As a famous and well-paid author, however, she enjoys an active social life in London, mixing especially with writers, artists, and theater people.

1898 After years of living separate lives, Frances and Swan Burnett are divorced; their son Vivian graduates from Harvard and initiates a career in journalism. Burnett begins a nine-year residence in Maytham Hall, Rolvenden, Kent. Playing the role of "lady of the manor," she elicits the love of her village neighbors with her generosity. At Maytham she turns a walled, overgrown orchard into a rose garden, where she often sits to write. In this garden she gets her first ideas for *The Secret Garden.*

1900 Newspapers headline Burnett's February marriage to Stephen Townesend, in Genoa, Italy; the marriage is unhappy, however, and Burnett separates from him after just two years.

1901 In *The Making of a Marchioness,* a short romance playfully based on the Cinderella story, Burnett satirizes the high-society marriage market.

1902 The play *A Little Princess,* another version of the Cinderella tale, based on "Sara Crewe" (1887), opens in London and, early the next year, in New York; its success is compared with that of the earlier *Little Lord Fauntleroy* (1886, 1888). Pauline Chase, who plays one of the school girls in the New York production of *A Little Princess,* will later star in James Barrie's *Peter Pan* (1904).

1904 Burnett writes to her friend Kate Douglas Wiggin to praise *Rebecca of Sunnybrook Farm* (1903); like *A Little Princess,* Wiggin's book features a girl with a highly developed imagination. Burnett's continuing grief over her son Lionel's death is reflected in *In the Closed Room,* portraying a dead child's attempts to let her surviving mother know that she is happy. The paradisiacal garden in which the dead child plays anticipates the association of the garden and death in *The Secret Garden.*

1905 The book *A Little Princess* builds on and expands the 1887 story "Sara Crewe" and the 1902 play. Burnett becomes a U.S. citizen.

1907 *The Shuttle,* a long adult romance about Anglo-American marriages, is so successful that it eventually pays for the Italianate villa Burnett builds at Plandome, Long Island.

1909 The fantasy parable *The Land of the Blue Flower* anticipates *The Secret Garden* by showing how gardening and good thoughts can transform a small society. Critics see Burnett's play *The Dawn of a To-morrow* as a tribute to the theology of Mary Baker Eddy, but she denies she is a Christian Scientist. She moves into her new home on Long Island, in the garden of which she will write much of *The Secret Garden.*

1910	*The Secret Garden* begins serialization in *The American Magazine.*
1911	*The Secret Garden* is published as a book; sales and critical attention do not forecast that it will become her most enduring work. She spends the first of many winters in Bermuda, where she plants a rose garden.
1912	*My Robin* describes how a bird in her earlier Maytham Hall garden had inspired her to create the robin who helps Mary in *The Secret Garden. Racketty-Packetty House,* based on the 1906–1907 *St. Nicholas Magazine* story and set to music by Burnett's son Vivian, opens a new Children's Theater in New York.
1913	*T. Tembarom,* a best-selling long romance for adults, retraces the outlines of the Little Lord Fauntleroy story, this time with a young adult protagonist. Burnett negotiates contracts to have several of her books adapted for the movies.
1914	Burnett makes her last return to the United States, aware that because of the war and its accompanying social changes, the Europe she has known is fast disappearing. She spends most of the rest of her life at Plandome and on Bermuda.
1915	Partly inspired by the role of Balkan unrest in precipitating World War I and likely influenced by Rudyard Kipling's *Kim* (1901), *The Lost Prince* portrays two children who assist a prince to recapture his hereditary throne; it gives a mystical cast to royalist nationalism and, in an uncomfortable reminder of Social Darwinism, suggests that some are born to be masters.
1916	Burnett enjoys being grandmother to Verity, the first of two daughters to be born to Vivian and his wife, Constance Buel Burnett.
1917	Dedicated to her son Lionel, who had died almost 30 years earlier, *The White People,* like *In the Closed Room* (1904), assures a parent that her dead child hovers happily nearby.
1922	Seventy-three-year-old Burnett publishes *The Head of the House of Coombe* and its sequel *Robin;* set against the background of World War I, these sentimental, melodramatic romances find a substantial audience but seem hopelessly dated

to critics now reading authors such as James Joyce, Virginia Woolf, and F. Scott Fitzgerald.

1924   Burnett makes her last public appearance at the opening of Mary Pickford's film version of *Little Lord Fauntleroy*. When she dies 29 October at Plandome, Burnett is remembered primarily as the author of that book published almost 40 years earlier.

1925   Written while she was propped up in bed during her last illness and now published posthumously, *In the Garden* expresses Burnett's love and knowledge of gardening. A refrain in this book is prophetic of the work for which she will eventually be most respected: "As long as one has a garden one has a future; and as long as one has a future one is alive."

LITERARY AND HISTORICAL
CONTEXT

1

The Secret Garden
and the Golden Age of Children's Literature

When *The Secret Garden* was published as a book in 1911, the first "Golden Age" of children's literature was already a half century old. By the 1850s and 1860s the earlier Romantic assertion that folk tales keep the child's imagination alive was resulting in adaptations of oral tales and literary fantasy, such as Nathaniel Hawthorne's *Wonder Book* (1852), William Makepeace Thackeray's *Rose and the Ring* (1855), Charles Kingsley's *Water Babies* (1863), and Lewis Carroll's *Alice in Wonderland* (1865). In addition, the prominence given child characters by novelists like Charles Dickens and the Brontë sisters was encouraging more complex character portrayal in realist books for the young, notably Thomas Hughes's *Tom Brown's School Days* (1857) and Louisa May Alcott's *Little Women* (1868–69).

THE JUVENILE ROMANCE

Frances Hodgson Burnett was growing up during these same two decades and began her publishing career near their end; in 1868, shortly before her nineteenth birthday, she published her first stories, in *Godey's Lady's Book,* which were followed by 15 years of critically acclaimed adult fiction. It was not until the early 1880s, as mother of two young sons, that she began to write for children, notably the book for which she would be best remembered when she died in 1924, *Little Lord Fauntleroy* (1886). The phenomenal international popularity of this Anglo-American Cinderella tale directed Burnett's career away from realist adult novels toward the popular romances for children and adults that brought her great wealth and fame but increasing disdain from the critics. In making this career redirection, Burnett was going against the stream of critical orthodoxy. During the 1880s Robert Louis Stevenson argued for the esthetic legitimacy of the romance and published two adventure romances that would become juvenile classics, *Treasure Island* (1883) and *Kidnapped* (1886); by the end of the century, however, the romance was largely relegated to the realm of popular literature. Here it was treated with critical condescension, the split between popular and "serious" literature having widened considerably by the end of the century.

Little Lord Fauntleroy had to swim against the current not only because of its genre but also, though somewhat later, because of its portrayal of the child, particularly the male child. With his ringlets, velvet and lace suits, and willingness to please others, especially adults, Burnett's little lord was the kind of boy reviled as a sissy by the rough-clad, adult-sparring heroes in Mark Twain's *Tom Sawyer* (1876) and *Huckleberry Finn* (1884). At first *Little Lord Fauntleroy* rode the tide of a late-nineteenth-century sentimentality about childhood, but its exceptional popularity made it a chief representative of that tide when it eventually crested. The book's resulting notoriety was in some ways unfair. Many readers aware of its reputation have been surprised to find its hero and story so engaging; moreover, the turn of the century saw books arguably more sentimental about childhood itself if not about their specific protagonists. In his autobiographically based *The Golden Age* (1895) and *Dream Days* (1898), for example, Kenneth Grahame suggested that children are in many ways superior to adults, as in their imaginative and playful enjoyment of life; Peter Pan's resolve never to grow up, in James Barrie's 1904 play, was a logical extension of Grahame's childhood memoirs.

By 1904 Burnett herself had had plenty of experience in the theater. She had adapted a considerable number of her works for the stage, including her 1888 play based on *Little Lord Fauntleroy*. In 1902 "Sara Crewe," a story that originally appeared in the children's publication *St. Nicholas Magazine* (1887), was turned into a play and in 1905 into a full-length book, both titled *A Little Princess*. An adaptation of the Cinderella tale, *A Little Princess* would eventually join *Little Lord Fauntleroy* and *The Secret Garden* as the trio of books on which Burnett's claims as a classic children's writer would ultimately rest.

BOOKS ABOUT ORPHAN GIRLS

In its portrayal of a spunky girl with a prodigious imagination, *A Little Princess* resembled two "girls' books" published during the same decade, Kate Douglas Wiggin's *Rebecca of Sunnybrook Farm* (1903) and L. M. Montgomery's *Anne of Green Gables* (1908). All of the protagonists in these books are orphans—Rebecca's mother is still alive but lacks the resources to educate her; all of the girls are given to the care of adults who, at least initially, find the child antipathetic. Mary Lennox's situation in *The Secret Garden,* published several years later, is similar. After her parents' death she joins the household of an uncle who wants little to do with her. Mary lacks the fanciful imagination of Sara, Rebecca, and Anne, however; unlike them, she is not winsome from the first. Indeed, the book's apparent intention that the reader find Mary and her cousin Colin initially disagreeable is often cited as path breaking among Golden Age classics, which tended to idealize the child.

In other ways, however, *The Secret Garden* continued earlier traditions. Much of the book's continuing appeal for young readers comes from its portrayal of the life children share away from adults. Just as Tom Sawyer and his friends had relished their secret life on Jackson's island, now Mary, Colin, and Dickon delight in keeping the mansion adults in the dark about their games and picnics in the garden. Taking her cue from Grahame's *The Golden Age,* Edith Nesbit had also focused on children's group adventures in her Bastable books, beginning with *The Story of the Treasure Seekers* (1899), and her fantasies, inaugurated with *The Five Children and It* (1902). And it can be argued that the lion, tin man, scarecrow, and Dorothy are all children making important discoveries about themselves without the assistance of adults in L. Frank Baum's *The Wizard of Oz* (1899).

THE ROMANTIC ASSOCIATION OF CHILDHOOD AND NATURE

Similarly found in other Golden Age classics are pastoral themes in *The Secret Garden* that link the children's healing with their work in the garden. The Romantic movement had often suggested that the child is especially close to nature. In his autobiographical *Prelude* (1805, 1850), for example, William Wordsworth had portrayed himself as a child often wandering alone among mountains and lakes, and he had called nature his first and best teacher. Somewhat later, Twain, Grahame, Wiggin, Montgomery, and others portrayed children as most happily themselves out of doors. Similarly, in Burnett's childhood memoir, *The One I Knew the Best of All* (1893), she had described how constricted she had felt in an inner-city Manchester square, how her imagination had been stimulated by an abandoned walled garden she found there as well as, later, by a thicket in rural Tennessee, where her family eventually settled.

If children were portrayed as especially appreciative of natural landscapes, they were also attributed a special affinity with animals and birds, such as Mary Lennox's robin. Anna Sewell's *Black Beauty* (1877) frankly appealed to children's compassion, and the turn of the century saw a burgeoning of more realistic animal stories such as those by Ernest Thompson Seton and Charles G. D. Roberts, as well as Jack London's best-seller, *Call of the Wild* (1903). Animal fantasies often portrayed more domesticated animals, as in two picture books published the same year as *The Call of the Wild:* Beatrix Potter's *Peter*

Rabbit and L. Leslie Brooke's *Johnny Crow's Garden*. Child and animal worlds were easily conflated in writers' imaginations. In his *Jungle Book* (1894) Rudyard Kipling imagined a boy being reared by wild animals, and in his *Wind in the Willows* (1909) Kenneth Grahame transposed his earlier childhood memoirs into animal fantasy. Grahame's fantasy shares with *The Secret Garden* a number of pastoral images and themes, including a fascination with Pan, the goat-footed Greek demi-god who had come to represent a union with nature often perceived to have been lost. In Grahame's book a lost baby otter finds refuge between the hoofs of Pan, the sight of which provides Rat and Mole a moment of mystical ecstasy. In *The Secret Garden* Pan appears as Dickon, who rescues baby lambs lost on the moor even as he helps save Mary and Colin by working with them in the garden.

SIGNS OF ITS TIME

Also like other Golden Age classics, *The Secret Garden* reflects some conventional social views of its time. If the portrayal of Mary and her interaction with the Sowerby family implies a certain uneasiness about a patriarchal class system, that system seems confirmed by Burnett's subsequent portrayal of Colin and his reforming father, who finally returns to take charge of his neglected heir and estate. A similar confirmation of the class system concludes *The Wind in the Willows,* when the friends of the irresponsible Toad try to reform him and fight to restore him to the inherited manor he, too, has neglected. Having protagonists reared in colonial India, both *The Secret Garden* and *A Little Princess* assume the empire background that Kipling explored more fully, for example in *Kim* (1901), which likely influenced Burnett's *The Lost Prince* (1915). In addition, aspects of the form of *The Secret Garden* may seem dated to many readers; being structured by the rebirths of Mary, Colin, and his father and including explicit statements of some of its themes, *The Secret Garden* was influenced by the earlier moral tale or exemplum, the overt didacticism of which has gone out of fashion.

Many readers, however, have apparently been able to overlook these features while appreciating the book's rich characterization, its mythic imagery and themes. It is these latter attributes that have allowed *The Secret Garden* to transcend its own era, engaging generations of child readers as well as adults longing to recapture some of the feelings of childhood.

2

The Secret Garden as a Classic

The importance of *The Secret Garden* can be gauged by its readership, its adaptation in other media, its influence on other writers, and the attention it has received from literary historians and critics. *The Secret Garden* has experienced an arc of readership opposite that of *Little Lord Fauntleroy,* which was phenomenally successful for several decades after which its readership gradually tapered off, though it maintained wide name recognition. By comparison, *The Secret Garden* was only moderately successful when it was published in 1911; and, over a decade later, at the time of Burnett's death in 1924, obituaries in the *New York Times* and the London *Times* remembered her for *Little Lord Fauntleroy* but did not mention *The Secret Garden.* A *New York Times* article the next day briefly referred to it as "The Secret Orchard."[1]

READERS LEAD THE CRITICS

A 1927 survey of more than 1,400 *Youth's Companion* readers, however, suggested that *The Secret Garden* was quietly finding its audience; it was in the top-15 list of "favorite books" named by 862 girls, although it did not make the boys' list.[2] Perhaps because its readership was—and has continued to be—predominantly female, *The Secret Garden* was not chosen by producers who were making film adaptations of a considerable number of other children's works during the 1930s, including *Little Lord Fauntleroy* and *A Little Princess*—neither of which appeared on the 1927 *Youth's Companion* lists of favorites. Not until 1949 was *The Secret Garden* made into a movie, starring Margaret O'Brien.

As late as 1960 there was still evidence that readers were ahead of official arbiters of taste in according the novel classic status. When the London *Sunday Times* published a list of the 99 best books for children, it was readers who overwhelmingly voted *The Secret Garden* as the hundredth.[3] The book's popularity with young readers by that time is confirmed by surveys during the 1970s and 1980s of adults' favorite childhood books. These, according to Jerry Griswold, "indicate that women, particularly, remember it among their favorite childhood books; only *Little Women* [the girls' favorite in the 1927 survey] is chosen more often."[4] The growth of university children's literature classes during this same period demonstrated that, like Burnett's other children's books in their time, *The Secret Garden* appeals to many adult as well as child readers. Alison Lurie, for example, found it to be the most popular book in her children's literature course at Cornell.[5]

During the last two decades *The Secret Garden* has received generous attention from literary critics (as described in the next chapter) and has often received the tribute of adaptation in other media. Movie versions appeared in 1975 (BBC television), in 1987 (CBS television), and in 1993 (Warner Brothers). In 1991 a children's opera by Nona Sheppard and Helen Glavin was performed in England, and an opera by Greg Plishka and David Ives premiered in Pennsylvania. In addition, *The Secret Garden* has twice been adapted for the musical stage. A 1983 British musical was short-lived; however, a Tony Award–winning musical by Marsha Norman and Lucy Simon held the Broadway stage from April 1991 through December of 1992, after which it had a successful, longer run on the road in the United States and abroad.

The Secret Garden *as a Classic*

THE BROAD INFLUENCE OF *THE SECRET GARDEN*

As a result of this continuing readership, adaptation, and attention in the popular media, the title of Burnett's classic, like that of *Little Lord Fauntleroy* earlier, is known by many who have not read the book, and the term *secret garden* is found in a surprising variety of contexts. Recent magazine articles, for example, have used it to apply to actual gardens of famous people, glass-bead jewelry, abstract paintings, a giftware store, an anti-cancer drug, teacher education classes, and one's recollections of childhood reading.[6] Following a tradition at least as old as medieval literature, the term sometimes has sexual connotations, as in Nancy Friday's widely read collection of women's erotic fantasies, *My Secret Garden* (1973). Especially since Jean-Jacques Rousseau's *New Eloise* (1761) and *Emile* (1762), paintings, poetry, fiction, and autobiography have often associated gardens with female domesticity and childhood.

Burnett's book, however, deserves much of the credit for keeping this symbolism alive in the twentieth century. In an essay describing how her recollection of her grandmother's garden was affected by gardens in books she has read, Anita T. Sullivan named Burnett's book as "perhaps most important"; read and reread by Sullivan during childhood and adulthood, *The Secret Garden* was "the pebble" that turned her "simple childhood experience into a pearl."[7] Similarly, in an essay on the garden as female symbol in various authors, Doris B. Wallace has suggested that Burnett's book contains "the most famous secret garden" not only in "children's literature" but "perhaps in Western European and North American literature."[8]

The influence of this children's book is to be found in some rather unlikely places. At least three scholars, apparently independently, have concluded that Burnett's book was an important source for the rose garden imagery in T. S. Eliot's *Four Quartets* (1943), and two other critics have described a surprising number of parallels between *The Secret Garden* and D. H. Lawrence's *Lady Chatterley's Lover* (1928).[9] Eliot would have been 23 and Lawrence 26 in 1911, when Burnett's book was published, supporting a common understanding that during the late nineteenth and early twentieth centuries readership of children's and adult books was not as segregated as it is today. Of the 32 "best-sellers" in the United States during the first 15 years of the twentieth century identified by Frank Luther Mott, at least eight would now be considered juvenile titles; Mott's list of "better sellers" for the same time period includes at least three more.[10]

INFLUENCE ON LATER FICTION FOR CHILDREN

A comprehensive survey of the influence of The Secret Garden on subsequent children's literature remains to be done; that such a study would be worthwhile, however, may be suggested by a few examples. In British writer Philippa Pearce's Tom's Midnight Garden (1958), often considered a classic, a boy, separated from his family like Mary Lennox, plays with a girl in a garden mysteriously tied to the past. In her more recent time-travel fantasy, The Root Cellar (1981), Canadian Janet Lunn explicitly alludes to The Secret Garden in her story of an orphan who is sent to live with her cousins. Finally, Katherine Paterson's Newbery Medal winner Bridge to Terabithia (1977) retold part of Burnett's story in a rural area just outside Washington, D.C.; as in Burnett's book, children find friendship, magic, death, and renewal in their own secret, sacred, natural place.[11] Not surprisingly, one of Paterson's favorite childhood books was The Secret Garden, which she has called "more a mystical experience than a book"; "it gives the harmony of Eden to the child reader"; "I think the reason so many of us have loved that book is precisely because we are homesick for a garden we have never visited."[12]

3

Critical Reception

When *The Secret Garden* was published as a book in 1911, most reviewers were appreciative, calling it "a very tender idyll," "wholesome," and "full of inspiration."[1] A considerable number of reviewers predicted that it would appeal to adults. Revealing some condescension toward children's fiction, one reviewer observed a "deep vein of symbolism" in *The Secret Garden,* which makes it "more than a mere story of children."[2] Another identified a "touch of the grown-up heart and experience . . . that makes it belong almost as much to general literature as to the literature of the schoolroom."[3] This potential appeal for adults undoubtedly contributed to its having been taken for serialization in *The American Magazine* the year before it appeared as a book—the first time in Burnett's recollection that a children's story had been thus featured in an adult magazine.[4] Praise for the book was not universal, however. An *Athenaeum* reviewer found *The Secret Garden* "over-sentimental and dealing almost wholly with abnormal people"; the book was labeled a "new-thought story," no doubt alluding to the role of positive thinking in the children's recovery; the reviewer found the book's "moral" "obvious" but opined that "the story will appeal to many women and young girls."[5]

LASKI'S 1951 REASSESSMENT

This kind of bias against books perceived as having a primarily female readership may have contributed to the decline in Burnett's reputation during the first half of the twentieth century. For decades after she died, Burnett was written about mainly as the originator of the Little Lord Fauntleroy "plague" with its "sissy" hero, according to Francis Molson's survey of Burnett criticism.[6] Critical recognition began to change in 1951, however, when Marghanita Laski published *Mrs. Ewing, Mrs. Molesworth and Mrs. Hodgson Burnett,* a short book reassessing the contributions of these near contemporary writers for children. Laski identified *Little Lord Fauntleroy, A Little Princess,* and *The Secret Garden* as Burnett's best books for children, the third being a "considerable advance" over the earlier two. Laski declared *The Secret Garden* "the most satisfying children's book I know," especially for "those introspective children at war with themselves and the world whom no other children's writer has ever helped and comforted."[7] Laski's assessment has lasted; none of Burnett's other books has been added to this trio, and of these, *The Secret Garden* has elicited by far the most attention from literary critics.

Laski's book inaugurated three decades during which *The Secret Garden* as well as Burnett's life and entire literary career were gradually rediscovered by literary historians and critics. Laski's high estimate of the book was not immediately picked up by others surveying and recommending children's books, however. Neither Burnett nor *The Secret Garden* appeared in the index of Lillian Smith's 1953 *The Unreluctant Years: A Critical Approach to Children's Literature,* for example, nor of Eleanor Cameron's 1962 *The Green and Burning Tree: On the Writing and Enjoyment of Children's Books.*[8] Roger Lancelyn Green omitted Burnett from his 1946 and 1953 versions of *Tellers of Tales;* in his preface to the 1953 version he did lament her exclusion, though he found room for chapters on Charlotte Yonge, Juliana Ewing, Mary Molesworth, and Edith Nesbit along with the usual male authors Lewis Carroll, George MacDonald, Robert Louis Stevenson, James Barrie, Rudyard Kipling, and Kenneth Grahame.[9] In a 1962 essay, however, Green noted the "astonishing staying power" of *The Secret Garden* and, echoing Laski, commented on its "unusual understanding of introspective, unlikable children."[10] Finally, in his 1965 *Tellers of Tales,* Green devoted much of a chapter to Burnett.[11] That same year, in the first edition of his influential history, *Written for Children,* John Rowe Townsend, found it "hard to account for" Burnett's "neglect by the critics," for, he acknowledged, "she has not been neglected by readers." Burnett is "now coming into her own," Townsend announced, and declared that she stands "far above every other woman writer for children except E. Nesbit; and there are depths in Mrs Hodgson Burnett that Nesbit never tried to plumb." This seems very high praise until one recalls that several pages earlier, speaking of Laski's book on Ewing, Molesworth, and Burnett, Townsend had said, "the grouping is reasonable enough so long as it does not mislead us into supposing that these writers were much of a muchness." These condescending comments disappeared in subsequent, revised editions of *Written for Children.*[12]

Thwaite's 1974 Biography

After Laski's book chapter, the next major milestone in Burnett criticism was Ann Thwaite's 1974 biography, *Waiting for the Party.* Biographies had been written earlier by two members of Burnett's family. In 1927, just three years after Burnett died, her son Vivian published the adulatory *Romantick Lady,* and in 1969 Vivian's wife, Constance Buel Burnett, published *Happily Ever After,* a children's biography based primarily on *Romantick Lady* and Burnett's own memoir, *The One I Knew The Best of All* (1893). Thwaite's well-researched and still-standard biography offered the most complete survey so far of Burnett's writing and theatrical career. Thwaite was more sympathetic than Laski to Burnett herself, whose private life and public persona had been somewhat controversial in her time; however, Thwaite lamented that Burnett had abandoned her early potential as a realist novelist to become a money-making machine, turning out popular romances for children and adults. Noting that

The Secret Garden has never been out of print, Thwaite called it ahead of its time for its portrayal of "actively disagreeable" children and for its being "astonishingly accurate to our own much greater understanding of child behavior." In addition, Thwaite noted the considerable number of parallels between *The Secret Garden* and Charlotte Brontë's *Jane Eyre*. In each, a young female orphan moves into a mansion in the Yorkshire moors and discovers a hidden occupant related to the master's unhappy past—a sick son in Burnett's book and a mad wife in Brontë. Thwaite declared that these parallels could hardly be "coincidental."[13]

Thwaite's 1974 biography of Burnett appeared as an increasing amount of scholarly attention was being paid to children's literature, women's literature, and popular culture. Because Burnett had made significant contributions to all three, she was ripe for reassessment. Indeed, it had already begun. In 1970 Robert Lee White had offered a revisionist account of the *Little Lord Fauntleroy* phenomenon, arguing that the little lord's reputation as a "prissy mollycoddle" misrepresents the book and that the alternate, more accepted, Huck Finn model of masculinity has not always proved salutary.[14] In 1972 the first issue of the annual journal *Children's Literature* had contained Alison White's article identifying *The Secret Garden* as a likely source for the rose garden imagery in T. S. Eliot's *Four Quartets*.[15] And, though published in 1975, Francis Molson's survey of Burnett's critical reception and call for a book-length study of her career had obviously been written before Thwaite's biography appeared.[16]

ACHIEVING STATUS AS A CLASSIC

The next several years saw a number of appreciative articles placing *The Secret Garden* within appropriate literary traditions and attempting to explain its continuing appeal. In my 1978 analysis of *Little Lord Fauntleroy, A Little Princess,* and *The Secret Garden,* I discussed how in her children's books Burnett adapted themes and forms from fairy tales and moral tales about exemplary children. I described what she owed to the earlier Romantic movement and, in *The Secret Garden,* to a long Western tradition of literary pastoral.[17] In a similar vein the next year, Stephen Roxburgh used Northrop Frye's categories to describe the book's mythic appeal, and in the same journal Rosemary Threadgold praised *The Secret Garden* for its characterization and encouragement of children's self-reliance.[18] In a 1980 essay reflecting on what the book had meant to her as a child, Madelon Gohlke discussed its themes of loss and death.[19] Finally, Fred Inglis's comments about *The Secret Garden* in his 1981 book on children's fiction indicate how much Burnett's stock had risen since the 1960s, when historians such as Green and Townsend had been uncertain about where to place her. Inglis included Burnett with Lewis Carroll, Rudyard Kipling, Arthur Ransome, William Mayne, and Philippa Pearce as "comparatively safe" nominations for an otherwise "uncertain list" of "great children's novelists." Acknowledging the influence of the Romantic movement and the Brontës on *The Secret Garden,* Inglis praised its utopian vision, its "pagan Garden of Eden" where "nature dissolves class."[20]

By the early 1980s, therefore, recognition of *The Secret Garden* as a classic had achieved critical orthodoxy; and in the years that followed, a considerable number of scholars continued this appreciative tradition by unfolding more of the book's imagery and themes. In a 1982 review essay, Elizabeth Francis described the secret garden as "internal" and "maternal space," as a hopeful transformation of the images of imprisonment that Sandra M. Gilbert and Susan Gubar, in *The Madwoman in the Attic* (1979), had identified as endemic in nineteenth-century literature by women.[21] Some of the same points were made in my 1984 book on Burnett, which explored the relationship between her children's and adult fiction while assessing her entire nondramatic career.[22] The next year Roderick McGillis discussed how the many secrets in the book stimulate the reader to imaginatively play with the text, and in 1986 Gillian Adams showed how secrets assist in the children's healing (1986).[23] Two years later, M. Sarah Smedman argued that by portraying the secret garden as a source of regeneration, the book allows children to experience sacred time and space, making their reading of it a ritual of hope.[24]

CRITICAL DEBATES ABOUT GENDER

Once a book receives critical recognition as a classic, its prominence often makes it a target for attack. Thus it is not surprising that also, during the 1980s, a significant number of scholars began to adopt a more critical stance toward *The Secret Garden*. In two articles juxtaposed in the 1983 issue of *Children's Literature,* Elizabeth Lennox Keyser and U. C. Knoepflmacher initiated a continuing debate about *The Secret Garden* and gender. Keyser articulated many female readers' disappointment that once Colin arrives on the scene, Mary gradually recedes into the background. Keyser argued that because Colin is never as interesting as was the earlier "contrary" Mary, the book's quality seriously declines. Building on insights from Thwaite's biography, Keyser suggested that this change of character focus in *The Secret Garden* reflected Burnett's own uneasiness about Mary's assertiveness in the first part of the book. Knoepflmacher agreed with Keyser about the split within Burnett between her masculine and feminine qualities, as they were defined at the time. Knoepflmacher compared Burnett's portrayal of Mary in *The Secret Garden* to the more unbridled expression of female aggression in one of Burnett's early fantasies for children, "Behind the White Brick" (1879).[25] In a 1987 article Lissa Paul built on Keyser's reading of *The Secret Garden,* lamenting that Mary does most of the work in the book's archetypal quest while Colin reaps most of the rewards.[26]

Partly in response to these gender critiques and more in line with Elizabeth Francis's discussion of *The Secret Garden* as a "version of feminist pastoral," my 1991 article argued that the garden and the cooperation of various characters rather than either Mary or Colin lie at the center of Burnett's book, which provides a near utopian vision of female nurturance. These points were reiterated in Adrian Gunther's 1994 article asserting that because "female energy is at all times predominant," Colin "never at any point displaces Mary" "in the real terms of the text."[27] In a 1994 article, however, I described how Marsha Norman's disappointment in Colin's laying claim to the secret garden in the latter part of Burnett's book led her to make Mary clearly the central character in her 1991 Broadway musical adaptation.

18

I also described how through on-stage ghosts from Mary's past, Norman identified Colin's dead mother as an important source of the healing magic at work in the story, an interpretation I had developed in my 1991 article.[28]

PSYCHOLOGICAL READINGS

The Secret Garden has received psychoanalytic as well as feminist readings. In 1990 Alison Lurie described Mary and Colin as "not just ordinary sulky or naughty" but "severely neurotic" children.[29] In 1992 Jerry Griswold suggested that because Colin's mother died shortly after giving birth to him, he experiences Oedipal guilt for having come between his parents. According to Griswold, Colin must overcome the "rivalrous Bad Father," Dr. Craven, before he can be reunited with his real father.[30] In 1990 clinical psychiatry professor Barbara Almond described how Mary and Colin move from "developmental arrest" to normal "latency" within the garden community, which functions as "therapeutic milieu" with Mother Sowerby as "psychoanalytic" "therapist." Almond also described the book's special appeal to prepubertal girls, citing especially the female sexuality metaphorically suggested by the enclosed garden.[31] And somewhat earlier, in 1987, Claudia Marquis used the theories of Sigmund Freud and Jacques Lacan to reveal how Burnett's text privileges upper-class, male experience. She argued that through its portrayal of Mary and the garden, Burnett's book takes a temporary holiday from late-Victorian ruling-class ideology only to have it be reaffirmed when "Master Colin" asserts his ownership of the garden and dominance over those who work within it.[32]

IDEOLOGICAL READINGS

Similarly focusing on the book's ideology, Heather Murray in 1985 had found *The Secret Garden* "disturbed as well as disturbing," an "unlikely candidate for the position of classic." Murray examined how the text tries to harmonize the contradiction between the natural, classless society within the garden and the hierarchical, patriarchal society endorsed in the book's conclusion.[33] Expanding on this argument, Jerry Phillips's 1993 article explored what the book reveals about Britain's empire ideology: through Mary, we see the alienation experienced by the colonial who returns home; Colin exhibits the "imperial ego" by taking charge of the garden experiments; and the garden itself is a landlord's image of "an ordered workforce, based on divided labor." According to Phillips, Burnett's text implicitly "rehabilitates empire by relocating it in rural England."[34]

It would be inaccurate to consider the appreciative and the more critical scholars just described as belonging to two armed camps. Few if any of the first group would deny that *The Secret Garden* reflects attitudes about gender and class we would like to believe we have put behind us; often, like Smedman or myself, such critics acknowledge these dated attitudes as they focus on strengths that help explain the book's continuing appeal.[35] On the other hand, critics who set themselves the task of unearthing the various ideologies in Burnett's text discover it to be amazingly fertile in in their hands. Marquis, for example, finds much about the intersection of language and gender identity in Burnett's portrayal of Mary and Colin;[36] and Murray acknowledges respect for the book's "power to harmonize discordancies, to quell its own rebellions."[37] Finally, it is likely that all the critics whose work I have described would name *The Secret Garden* as the best of Burnett's books and, if not among the best, then certainly among the most important children's books written during the late nineteenth and early twentieth centuries.

THE EPITOME OF ITS ERA

Grudging testimony to this importance was paid by a critic notably unsympathetic to Burnett. In his 1985 study of this era in children's literature, Humphrey Carpenter provided only sporadic, condescending comments about Burnett's work; nevertheless, he borrowed from her the title of his book, *Secret Gardens: A Study of the Golden Age of Children's Literature.* Arguing that the chief identifying theme of this literature was an idealization of childhood as an "Arcadia, the Enchanted Place, the Never Never Land, the Secret Garden," Carpenter called Burnett's book the "work of fiction which, more clearly than any other single book, describes and celebrates the central symbol" of this "movement in English writing for children."[38]

A READING

4

"Mistress Mary, Quite Contrary"
(Chapters 1–8)

Burnett's first title for *The Secret Garden* was *Mistress Mary Quite Contrary,* and in her three short, introductory chapters she establishes indelibly how Mary Lennox is "contrary" and why. To do so, Burnett makes generous use of repetition, a literary device typically more obvious in children's than adult literature. The book's opening paragraph, for example, abundantly illustrates Burnett's use of verbal repetition. We are told that Mary "had a *little thin* face and a *little thin* body, *thin* hair and a sour expression"; that "her hair was *yellow,* and her face was *yellow* because she had been born in India and had always been ill in one way or another"; that "when she was a *sickly, fretful,* ugly little baby she was *kept out of the way,* and when she became a *sickly, fretful* toddling thing she was *kept out of the way* also" (emphasis added).[1] Burnett etches Mary's character through not only verbal but also conceptual repetition. Picking up on the idea that Mary has been "kept out of the way," Burnett reiterates how the girl is isolated, physically and geographically, psychologically and socially.

PHYSICAL AND GEOGRAPHICAL ISOLATION

Burnett especially emphasizes Mary's physical isolation, which provides what T. S. Eliot called an "objective correlative" for her psychological and social isolation—symbolic portrayal of character is particularly important for children's writers, who, unlike novelists for adults, cannot afford extended passages of abstract psychological analysis, especially in early chapters that must set the direction of the plot to draw young readers in. In Burnett's first chapter, "There Is No One Left," nine-year-old Mary is alone in her Indian bungalow except for a harmless little snake, for her parents have died of cholera and all the servants have died or fled—even the snake is scurrying to get out of her room (1:6). Physical isolation is not new to Mary. Her party-loving mother "had not wanted a little girl at all, and when Mary was born she handed her over to the care of an Ayah who was made to understand that . . . she must keep the child out of sight as much as possible" (1:1). The Ayah apparently did this job well, for the soldiers who now discover Mary declare that "no one ever saw her," and we later learn that "many people never knew that . . . [Mrs. Lennox] had a child at all" (1:6, 2:11).

Unfortunately, it appears that this physical isolation will continue, for when she arrives at the home of her uncle, Archibald Craven, in Yorkshire, England, she learns that he does not want to see her and will be leaving for London in the morning. Moreover, Mary is told that she must keep to her own two rooms, an isolation underscored by these rooms' being surrounded by almost 100 others, most of which are "shut up and locked" (1:23, 14). This isolation within Misselthwaite Manor is reinforced by the manor's geographical isolation. To reach it, Mary has had to travel through a long stretch of moors which, especially at night, had seemed so bare as to remind her of the sea she had just crossed to reach England (3:21). Burnett's extended description of Mary's journey reminds us that Mary is not only isolated but also dislocated, geographically and culturally, as is illustrated in a poignant scene before she left India. Having been told that she is to be "sent home," she had asked, "Where is home?" (2:9).

"Mistress Mary, Quite Contrary" (Chapters 1–8)

PSYCHOLOGICAL AND SOCIAL ISOLATION

In this context, of course, "home," had meant England, of which Mary has had no experience. In addition, however, she has had little experience of the smaller home where one learns to establish close human ties. That her isolation has been emotional as well physical is effectively dramatized by her reaction when she is told that her nurse and parents are dead. She does not cry; instead of grief, she expresses injured pride, stamping her foot and demanding of the soldiers who find her why no one has come to take care of her (1:5–7). Having lacked caregivers genuinely interested in her, Mary has in turn "never cared much for any one" else (1:5); the human bond most meaningful to her is that between master and servant, a bond characterized less by affection than control.

Mary's class prejudice reinforces her psychological and social isolation. When her uncle's housekeeper, Mrs. Medlock, escorts her to Yorkshire, Mary walks apart because she considers the woman's face and bonnet "common" and does "not want to seem to belong to her" (2:13). Earlier, she had been disdainful of the "shabby clothes" and "untidy bungalow" of the clergyman's family with whom she had stayed temporarily in India; she had "turned her face away when Mrs. Crawford attempted to kiss her, and [had] held herself stiffly when Mr. Crawford patted her shoulder" (2:8, 10). Similarly, she had told the Crawfords' son to "go away" when he wanted to join her play; when she refused his suggestions for the garden she was making with "heaps of earth," he sang the nursery rhyme later used as a taunt by the other Crawford children as well:

> Mistress Mary, quite contrary,
> How does your garden grow?
> With silver bells, and cockle shells,
> And marigolds all in a row. (2:9)

PSYCHOLOGICAL ADAPTATIONS

By being so "self-absorbed" and "disagreeable" (1:8, 12), Mary obviously increases her own isolation. Given her present circumstances, however, her contrariness can also be seen as an adaptive defense, a crucial survival tactic, as Elizabeth Lennox Keyser and U. C. Knoepflmacher have pointed out.[2] Affection for temporary caregivers and siblings only leads to pain when they are gone. And why should she invest hope in a future over which she has so little control? When the housekeeper, Mrs. Medlock, asks if she does not care about the Yorkshire destination being described to her, Mary declares, with some accuracy, "It doesn't matter . . . whether I care or not" (2:15). Given that everything in her life seems unstable and outside of her control, Mary's most important survival task is to tend to herself, to cultivate her own garden. Thus Mary's abortive attempts to create a garden in these early chapters—alone in her bungalow during the cholera epidemic (1:2) as well as later with the Crawfords—suggest that while her isolation has for the most part proved deleterious, it has also taught her to be independent. And it is Mary's contrary independence that will eventually impel her to find and enter the secret garden, despite being told it is forbidden.

While the first three chapters emphasize Mary's isolation and independence, they also contain indications that she may eventually reach out to others. Before being motivated to do so, of course, she must recognize her isolation as a lack, and this is precisely what happens when she is exposed to family life different from her own. Having observed not only the clergyman's family but also the officer's wife and children who accompanied her on the boat, Mary has "begun to wonder why she had never seemed to belong to any one even when her father and mother had been alive. Other children seemed to belong to their fathers and mothers, but she had never seemed to really be any one's little girl." Recognition of this lack is accompanied by an apparently new emotion. She "had begun to feel lonely" (2:12).

Mary is being prepared to acknowledge feelings appropriate to her situation not only through contact with others unlike herself but also by hearing about someone very much like herself. During the coach trip to Misselthwaite, Mrs. Medlock describes Mary's uncle as being as physically, emotionally, and socially isolated as she is. He "cares about nobody. He won't see people. Most of the time he goes away, and when he is at Misselthwaite he shuts himself up in the West Wing and won't let any one but [his personal servant] Pitcher see him." It is Mary's typical "intention not to seem to care," but when she hears that her uncle's wife died, she gives "a little involuntary jump" and, "quite without meaning to," exclaims, "Oh! did she die?" She, too, has lost family members, though as yet she can acknowledge her grief only indirectly, as it is reflected in another. Moreover, she quickly defends herself against that grief by rationalizing that it was because her uncle reminded her of a fairy tale about "a poor hunchback and a beautiful princess" that she felt "suddenly sorry" for him. And she soon reverts to her contrary egocentricity. Told that her uncle will not allow her to explore his house, Mary decides he is "unpleasant enough to deserve all that had happened to him" (2:15–17). Mary's mental, verbal, and behavioral reactions to her isolation in these first three chapters help explain why writers such as biographer Ann Thwaite and psychiatrist Barbara R. Almond have praised *The Secret Garden* for its psychological subtlety, even clinical accuracy.[3] Burnett had shown a similar psychological insight in her own memoir, *The One I Knew the Best of All: A Memory of the Mind of a Child* (1893).

YORKSHIRE THERAPY

Almond has described as "therapistlike" some of the characters Mary encounters in Yorkshire.[4] The first is the housemaid Martha Sowerby, who greets Mary the first morning she awakens in Misselthwaite Manor and elicits the child's first direct expression of grief for all that she has lost. The Yorkshire maid achieves this feat simply by expressing her own thoughts and feelings so forthrightly—"it is a Yorkshire habit to say what you think with blunt frankness," Burnett's narrator later observes, and Mary "had never heard the truth about herself in her life" (4:40). Martha speaks familiarly to the child and has a "sturdy way" that suggests that she might "even slap back" if Mary slapped her, as she had done to her Ayah when she had been angry (4:25). Further reminding Mary of the distressing unfamiliarity of her new surroundings, Martha speaks a dialect Mary does not always understand and confides disappointment that she is not one of the Indian "blacks" she has read about in religious tracts (4:27).

Given the hierarchical social values Mary has been taught, and given that her place near the top of this hierarchy is about the only sense of power she has, Mary considers it a grievous "humiliation" that Martha had thought she might be a "native." "You know nothing about India," Mary shouts, and her "rage" creates a chink in her self-control that allows her to throw "herself face down on the pillows and burst into passionate sobbing," to cry—at last—about being "so horribly lonely and far away from everything she understood and which understood her" (4:27–28).

Like a good therapist, Martha acknowledges the appropriateness of Mary's feelings—"I don't know anythin' about anythin'—just like you said"—but refuses to be manipulated by them. Mary must take some responsibility for herself and learn that good human relationships involve reciprocity. Martha will help Mary put on her dress, especially if it has buttons down the back, but Mary must put on her own shoes. Moreover, Martha suggests that Mary see her problems in a broader perspective. When the child refuses to eat her breakfast, Martha says that her own 11 siblings "scarce ever had their stomachs full in their lives" (4:28–31).

While Martha's frank demeanor and speech force Mary to acknowledge the foreignness of her new environment, they also elicit her curiosity. As Martha prattles on about her family, Mary begins "to feel a slight interest" in Martha's brother Dickon, who has a special affinity with animals; as Mary "had never before been interested in any one but herself," Burnett's narrator reminds us, this interest is "the dawning of a healthy sentiment" (4:31). Some chapters later, Martha uses Mary's interest in Dickon to teach her the importance of self-acceptance. When Mary says that she does not think Dickon would like her, since "no one does," Martha asks, "How does tha' like thysel'?" "Not at all—really," Mary answers, "but I never thought of that before" (7:62–63). Martha assures her that she is indeed likable by reporting that her siblings had been fascinated by her description of Mary, and Martha has returned from home with a "skippin'-rope" for Mary, purchased with her own wages (8:70–71). This gift of a skipping rope is one reason, no doubt, that Almond labels Martha an "occupational therapist."[5] In addition, it is Martha who, during Mary's first morning at Misselthwaite, tells Mary about the walled garden her uncle locked after his wife died, a mysterious secret that sends Mary outside to explore this new, foreign territory.

VERBALIZATION AND SELF-KNOWLEDGE

Almond observes that much as in the "therapeutic milieu" of a mental hospital, Mary has a number of "therapists" who work in tandem. During her first walk outside she meets another, the gardener, Ben Weatherstaff, who, along with a robin, helps Mary learn more about herself. Ben tells her that the robin is "lonely" because all the rest of its brood have flown away (4:38–39). Earlier, when Mary had seen her own isolation mirrored in Mrs. Medlock's description of Archibald Craven, she had not been ready to consciously recognize that resemblance. The encounter with Martha, however, has encouraged her to acknowledge her feelings. "I'm lonely," Mary says, and the narrator's next comment demonstrates considerable insight into the role of language in the development of self-awareness, a role that undergirds the efficacy of talk therapy. Mary "had not known before that this was one of the things which made her feel sour and cross" (4:39–40). At least twice before, Mary has been described as being lonely (2:12, 4:28), but this is the first time Mary has named the feeling for herself; having named it, she can see its relationship to other feelings, such as being "sour and cross."

Like Martha earlier, the gardener Ben helps Mary see that her feelings are appropriate to her situation, saying "Art tha' th' little wench from India? . . . Then no wonder tha'rt lonely." Also, as if psychoanalytically trained, Ben encourages Mary to transfer her feelings onto him, where she can look at them more objectively: "I'm lonely mysel'," he admits and then adds, "tha' an' me are a good bit alike. . . . We're neither of us good-lookin' and we're both of us as sour as we look. We've got the same nasty tempers, both of us, I'll warrant" (4:40). As with the robin, this mirroring has the desired therapeutic effect: "She had never thought much about her looks, but she wondered if she was as unattractive as Ben Weatherstaff, and she also wondered if she looked as sour as he had looked before the robin came. She actually began to wonder also if she was 'nasty-tempered'" (4:40–41).

THE MIND-BODY CONNECTION

In the chapters before Mary actually enters the secret garden, her changes are physical as well as psychological. Indeed, for Burnett, who was much influenced by Christian Science and the late nineteenth-century "new thought" movement, the two are integrally related. Much of this mind-body connection in the early chapters of *The Secret Garden* is expressed through Mary's relationship to food, which often reflects her psychosocial situation. Burnett here seems to anticipate our later identification and analysis of eating disorders like anorexia, especially prevalent in girls.

Early descriptions of Mary emphasize her thinness, and, in the first chapter, we see her helping herself to the "partly finished meal" abandoned by her parents before they died, much as she had earlier had to feed on their leftover affection (1:4–5). In part, Mary's thinness reflects others' lack of genuine interest in her. In part, also, her lack of appetite suggests her lack of interest in herself and her own fate, as when Martha has to urge her to eat. After Martha and Ben have taken a genuine interest in Mary, however, and after her quest to find the secret garden has excited her interest in her own life, she awakens one morning "knowing what it . . . [is] to be hungry" (5:45). Mary's appetite is stimulated also, of course, by her physical exertion in the fresh air. Burnett's description of this effect emphasizes the intimate relationship between body and mind. The same wind that "whipped some red colour into her cheeks" also begins "to blow the cobwebs out of her young brain and to waken her up a little" (5:44, 48).

BEGINNING TO FEEL AT HOME

Before Mary enters the garden, she has not only made significant psychological and physical improvements but is well on the way toward overcoming her geographical and cultural dislocation. She discovers that she prefers the English climate: "In India she had always felt hot and too languid to care much about anything" (5:48); "in India skies were hot and blazing." Now, however, she appreciates the beauty of the Yorkshire moor and "deep cool blue" sky (7:60). And she begins to identify Misselthwaite Manor as her home, as is symbolically suggested by Burnett's portrayal of a rainy-day exploration inside. Walking through a gallery of portraits, Mary at first feels like an intruder. "She felt as if . . . [the people in the portraits] were wondering what a little girl from India was doing in their house"; however, she finds two portraits of "a stiff, plain little girl like herself" (6:55–56). Just as seeing aspects of herself mirrored in Ben and the robin had helped her feel she belonged in their company, finding herself pictured in the manor now suggests that she belongs there as well.

A set of ivory elephants in another room serves as a reminder of her past life in India; however, after playing with the elephants for some time, she gets "tired" of them, carefully sets them back in their cabinet, and shuts the door. In contrast, she wishes she could take with her a mouse with its six babies she finds nested inside a sofa cushion (6:57–58). The living present is now preferable to the dead past; also, perhaps she now hopes to feel as comfortably at home inside the manor as do the family of mice.

JOURNEYS INTO THE UNCONSCIOUS

Citing the precedent of Edgar Allan Poe's "Fall of the House of Usher," Jerry Griswold has argued that Mary's indoor explorations suggest her probing of her unconscious and her seeking out secrets from her family past.[6] The fact that she finds the ivory elephants in what was once "a lady's sitting room," undoubtedly much like her mother's, does suggest an unconscious visit into her own past (6:57). And, of course, the portraits represent a family past to which she herself belongs, her father being a brother to Archibald Craven's wife. In addition, near the end of this indoor journey Mary hears a "fretful, childish whine" (6:58). As we learn later, it is the cry of her invalid cousin Colin, the family secret she has not yet discovered. But it can also suggest her own grieving self finally being heard from some unconscious recess. The 1993 movie adaptation embroidered these familial connections and psychological overtones. Mary plays with ivory elephants in the boudoirs of both her mother and Colin's dead mother, whom the movie portrays as sisters; and in a dream Mary envisions herself as a toddler crying in woodland foliage while her mother is whisked away by the wind.

In the book Mary's outdoor journeys to find the secret garden can similarly be interpreted as psychological explorations. Burnett links the two kinds of journeys by describing the estate gardens as a series of interlocking, walled rooms (4:34). Mary's intense interest in the garden's role in Mrs. Craven's death, for example, might stem partially from an unconscious conflation of that death with her mother's, neither death she herself having witnessed. More consciously, Mary connects the garden with herself; told by Ben Weatherstaff that no one has been inside it for ten years, she reflects that "she had been born ten years ago" (7:65). Being walled, locked, and abandoned, the garden mirrors her own well-defended, isolated, and orphaned self. Mary reflects that "it was because it had been shut up so long that she wanted to see it." Although Mary is well on her way toward breaking out of her earlier, unhealthy forms of psychological and social isolation, she needs a private place she can control. Mary considers that "she could go into it every day and shut the door behind her, . . . and play . . . quite alone, because nobody would ever know where she was. . . . The thought of that pleased her very much" (8:68).

"Mistress Mary, Quite Contrary" (Chapters 1–8)

FOLK-TALE MOTIFS

As has been suggested by this discussion of the psychological subtlety and depth of Burnett's portrayal of Mary, the first eight chapters fulfill many of the expectations we bring to a realist novel. Burnett's emphasis on journeys in these chapters, however—journeys from India to England, across the moors, on the estate grounds, and inside Misselthwaite Manor—invite us to read *The Secret Garden* also like a folk tale or romance, as is increasingly obvious as the book progresses. A comparison of Mary's adventures to those in such stories is suggested by the tapestries in Mary's Misselthwaite room, which depict a medieval hunting party and make her feel "as if she were in the forest with them" (4:24). Burnett was indeed much influenced by fairy tales, her two other best-known children's classics, *Little Lord Fauntleroy* (1886) and *A Little Princess* (1905), being adaptations of the Cinderella tale. While not so obvious in *The Secret Garden,* fairy-tale motifs often lie not too far below its story surface as well. In the first chapter Burnett's description of Mary awakening in a silent house filled with reminders of life abruptly interrupted might make some readers recall "The Sleeping Beauty"; later, after her Yorkshire life is beginning its transformation of Mary, she herself thinks of that tale, after which Burnett's narrator says "she was becoming wider awake every day which passed at Misselthwaite" (10:90).

In addition, by exhibiting the animistic, magical thinking typical of young children, Mary implicitly interprets her experience as if she were living in a folk tale, which often portrays a similar worldview. Mary easily slips into Ben Weatherstaff's habit of regarding the robin as human, for example, and she subsequently decides that the robin shows her how to get into the garden, first by pecking the earth next to where the key is buried and then by similarly directing her attention to a portion of the wall just as a gust of wind lifts the ivy to reveal a doorknob and keyhole. Being reminded of her Ayah's stories, Mary declares the assistance of the robin and wind to be "Magic" (7:66, 8:76).

A similarly minded reader might also describe as "Magic" how the wind had earlier pointed Mary toward Misselthwaite Manor's secret room. Because the wind had simultaneously opened her bedroom door and another elsewhere in the house, Mary had been able to hear "someone crying," someone not a "grown-up person" (5:49–51). Once that secret room's occupant joins Mary in the secret garden, "Magic" will be the children's label for the transformations they observe in the garden and themselves. First, however, Mary will explore the secret garden herself, alone.

5

"Might I Have a Bit of Earth?"
(Chapters 9–12)

Chapters 9–11 continue to focus on the stages of Mary's development; in addition, especially in Burnett's portrayal of the secret garden and other characters closely related to it, there are increasing indications that this is a book to be appreciated for symbolism and mythic resonance as well as psychological subtlety.

MARY AS GARDENER AND GARDEN

Often, to help measure how much Mary has grown, readers are invited to recall scenes from earlier in the book. When Mary first enters the garden, for example, she is especially struck by its isolation: "Everything was strange and silent and she seemed to be hundreds of miles away from everyone." Unlike the isolation she experienced earlier, however, this is a healthy isolation: "Somehow she did not feel lonely at all." In addition, what she does there suggests that she is beginning to take charge of her own life. She immediately regards the garden as "her new kingdom" (9:80, 82); she later gives it a name, "the Secret

Garden," and argues that "nobody has any right to take it from me when I care about it and they don't" (10:90, 102).

Mary's abortive attempts to create gardens in India had suggested an incipient ability to nurture herself. That she is now ready to do so is suggested by her instinctive knowledge of what the secret garden needs—as described in the previous chapter, the garden appeals to her in part because she sees it, however unconsciously, as a mirror of herself. She clears away dead weeds so that living shoots can "breathe"; accidently digging up a bulb, she does not know what it is but carefully puts it back in place (9:81, 82–83). Like Mary when we first saw her, the garden is now apparently dead; its few green points are like the signs of life once hidden inside Mary but now nurtured to the surface by the "gardeners" Martha and Ben. That Mary is now both gardener and garden, nurturing herself even as she is being nurtured, is suggested also by a comparison of Mary herself to a bulb or a shoot. We are told that Mary "surprised" Ben "several times by seeming to start up beside him as if she sprang out of the earth" (10:91), a description that recalls Martha's earlier assertion that bulbs are "things as helps themselves. . . . If you don't trouble 'em, most of 'em'll work away underground for a lifetime" (9:83).

REACHING OUT TO OTHERS

Finding the secret garden and learning to care for herself better make Mary self-confident enough to trust others, to ask for help, and to share. In India she had told the clergyman's son, Basil, to go away when he offered a suggestion about the pretend garden she was making out of heaps of dirt. Now, through Martha, Mary asks Dickon Sowerby to purchase some garden tools for her, and when he brings them she invites him inside the garden to help her tend it. Burnett suggests that the reader compare these two gardening scenes by having Mary tell Dickon about how Basil and his siblings had taunted her with the nursery rhyme, "Mistress Mary, quite contrary, / How does your garden grow?" (11:110). Basil and Dickon also have a number of similarities; each comes from a poor family with numerous children, each has blue eyes and a "turned-up" nose, and each is a boy—a point especially noted in each scene (2:9, 10:97).

Mary's contrasting reaction to Basil and Dickon indicates that the company of Martha and Ben has given her a new perspective on social class. While she had been disdainful of Mrs. Medlock's "common" face and Basil's "shabby" clothes, she now immediately likes Dickon, although he is "only a common moor boy, in patched clothes" (2:13, 8, 10:99). In fact, she wishes she were like him. She admires and tries to use his Yorkshire dialect, and she wishes she had a big mouth just like his (12:115). Mary has also learned from Martha and Ben the "Yorkshire habit" of "plain speaking" (4:40). "I like you," she tells Dickon, and she is willing to risk rejection by adding, "Does tha' like me?" (11:111, 112).

LATENT SEXUALITY

The fact that she likes and is liked by a boy represents a significant change in Mary. When she had told Basil to "go away" from her pretend garden, she had added, "I don't want boys" (2:9). When Mary first meets Dickon, Burnett's narrator tells us that "Mary knew nothing about boys and she spoke to him a little stiffly because she felt rather shy," and just before Mary trusts Dickon with her secret she herself says, "I don't know anything about boys" (10:98, 101).

In her analysis of the special appeal of *The Secret Garden* for a prepubertal girl "between 9 and 11 years old"—Mary's age—psychiatrist Barbara R. Almond says that the book "deals with the issue that is uppermost on her mind—the development of her own sexuality and femininity as she approaches puberty." Providing a more sexual cast to the book's symbolic connection between the secret garden and Mary herself, Almond says that the garden "may represent the female genital, a hidden place that must be opened up and planted. It is also a place where feminine roles can be learned and rehearsed." "Despite successful sublimation," Almond asserts, "latency-age children are highly invested in their sexual feelings and theories, and need to share them and play them out with other children."[1] Ten-year-old Mary's inviting 12-year-old Dickon to join her play in the garden thus represents significant psychosexual development.

Indeed, the sensuous relationship with nature that Mary and Dickon share in the secret garden often suggests the sublimated, polymorphous, pregenital sexuality during latency, as has been pointed out by Judith Plotz as well as Almond.[2] Mary tells Dickon, "I like to smell the earth when it's turned up," to which he replies that he likes to "lie under a bush an' listen to th' soft swish o' [rain] drops on the heather an' . . . just sniff an' sniff" (11:108). On occasion, their excitement almost sounds like mutual sexual exploration as when Mary "quite panted with eagerness, and Dickon was eager as she was. They went from tree to tree and from bush to bush. Dickon carried his knife in his hand and showed her things which she thought wonderful" (11:106).

The sexual overtones of chapters 9–12 are further enhanced by Burnett's portrayal of the male robin, one of only two "persons" (the other is Dickon) Mary identifies as so far liking her (11:112). The robin—as described by a gardener whose last name, Weatherstaff, contains a phallic reminder of his sex—is almost a caricature of masculine courtship. After Mary has observed how the robin has strutted and "flirted his wings," Ben Weatherstaff tells the bird, "I know what tha's up to. Tha's courtin' some bold young madam somewhere, tellin' thy lies to her about bein' the finest cock robin on Missel Moor an' ready to fight all th' rest of 'em" (10:93). This is the same robin, of course, who had earlier courted Mary. By helping her find the key and door, he had invited her into the secret garden, the place where he was born, reared, and now lives (4:37–38).

CONFRONTING PATRIARCHAL AUTHORITY

While masculinity in the form of a bird or another child is pleasing to Mary, a male adult guardian is clearly more threatening. Being told that she must see her uncle precipitates a temporary regression: "Her heart began to thump and she felt herself changing into a stiff, plain, silent child again" (12:117). She really is not, however, the same girl who, a little over a month ago on her way to Misselthwaite, had decided she would not like Mr. Craven (10:92, 4:36). Having learned from observing Ben Weatherstaff's face that one's feelings can affect one's looks, she now considers her uncle "not ugly"; in fact, "his face would have been handsome if it had not been so miserable" (12:118). Being far less self-absorbed than she was earlier, she can recognize that though he is distracted and knows little about children, her uncle wishes her well. As a result, she has the courage to ask him for what she wants: more time playing out of doors to get stronger before having a governess and, most important, permission to tend the secret garden, which she had earlier told Dickon she had "stolen" (10:102). "Might I have a bit of earth?" she asks her uncle. And by getting him to agree that she may take the "earth" "from anywhere—if it's not wanted," she cleverly gets his permission to tend the garden he himself had locked and forbidden, and without revealing her secret (12:121).

Mythic Allusions

Burnett underscores the parallel transformations of Mary and the garden through an archetypal use of the seasonal cycle. Mary had arrived in late winter, the season often associated with death. Now, when a changing Mary enters the secret garden about a month later, the green shoots provide the promise of spring, the season typically associated with rebirth.

Also derived from myth is the boy who assists Mary in the secret garden. In her portrayal of Dickon, Burnett recalls Pan, the Greek god of shepherds and goatherds. Pan was a nature deity who had the horns and hoofs of a goat, loved wild places, and played a reed pipe while woodland nymphs danced. As such, Pan has often represented an ideal unity of human beings with nature—he is interpreted thus in Kenneth Grahame's *The Wind in the Willows* (1909) as well as in *The Secret Garden,* serialized just a year later. In addition, because Pan was often in pursuit of nymphs, he has sometimes been an icon of sexuality—as has been suggested, Dickon can be seen as playing this role as well in Burnett's book.

Dickon's resemblance to Pan is obvious when Mary first sees him. Sitting under a tree, he is playing "a rough wooden pipe" to the rapt attention of a squirrel, a cock pheasant, and some rabbits (10:97). He lacks distinguishing physical features like Pan's horns and hoofs; his hybrid nature is suggested by traits more consistent with the book's predominantly realist mode. He spends most of his time on the moors with wild animals; he can converse with animals and birds, acting as translator between Mary and the robin (10:100). Thus, like Pan, Dickon seemingly belongs to several orders of being at once. "Sometimes I think p'raps I'm a bird, or a fox, or a rabbit, or a squirrel, or even a beetle, an' I don't know it," he tells Mary, and he later describes himself as behaving like a rabbit (10:101, 11:108). He has a special identity with the vegetable world as well; Mary notices "a clean fresh scent of heather and grass and leaves about him, almost as if he were made of them"; accordingly, he can give Mary expert advice on how to tend the secret garden (10:99).

Dickon's hybrid nature calls attention to how Burnett blurs the lines between human and nonhuman creatures elsewhere. The robin is personified not only by Ben, Mary, and Dickon, but also by Burnett's narrator, who at one point tells us what the robin thought about Ben and Mary (9:82). In addition, as has been noted, Martha personifies bulbs under the ground, and Burnett's narrator describes Mary as if she were a bulb shooting up through the earth. Finally, with his resemblance to Pan, Dickon reminds us that Burnett's book itself is a hybrid combination of realist fiction with myth and folk tale. Mary herself recognizes that Dickon belongs as much to the realm of fabulous stories as to the everyday world. After their first visit in the garden, she considers Dickon "too good to be true" and wonders "if he might be a sort of wood fairy" (11:113). Later, returning to find the garden empty, she again wonders if Dickon "was only a wood fairy"—until she finds a note saying, "I will cum bak" (12:123). Before the two meet again in the garden, however, Mary will have discovered within Misselthwaite Manor a secret room with contents as surprising if not as immediately pleasant as those she found in the secret garden.

6

"I Am Colin" (Chapters 13–20)

During her month at Misselthwaite, Mary Lennox has occupied herself with two forbidden quests that are in many ways parallel. So far, Burnett has concentrated primarily on the girl's journey through walled gardens to find the locked, abandoned secret garden. Chapter 13 now depicts the conclusion to Mary's journey through the manor's corridors to find a secret room with its virtually abandoned resident—her invalid cousin, Colin Craven. In addition to having the parallels suggested by this description, Mary's two quests have some significant contrasts.

MARY'S JOURNEY BACKWARD

Mary's journeys to find the the secret garden had occurred out of doors and during the daytime, primarily when it was sunny. In this book health depends on fresh air and sunlight, and Burnett has described the healing of both Mary and the garden as an "awakening" (9:79, 10:90). If Mary's outdoor, daytime explorations suggest progression, her indoor, nighttime journeys to find her cousin Colin are in some ways regressive, retracing her steps backward from health to illness, from waking to sleeping. In chapter 5 Mary's first attempt to locate the source of the mysterious cry had occurred when rain had kept her indoors. Now, in chapter 13, a rainstorm awakens her at night, and when her search of dark corridors leads to Colin's hidden room, both children think they might still be asleep—each at first thinks that the other is either a "ghost" or a "dream" (13:127–28).

Like the garden earlier, 10-year-old Colin now provides a mirror for 10-year-old Mary. Like Mary, Colin has suffered parental abandonment and neglect: his mother died when he was born, and his grief-stricken father finds seeing him so painful that he visits him primarily at night when the boy is asleep. While green shoots in the garden had made it a hopeful image of what Mary was already becoming, however, Colin confronts her with an exaggerated picture of what she once was. While Mary had been merely "sickly" (1:1), Colin is apparently unable to walk and believes that he will die before he grows up. Colin's isolation is similarly more excessive than hers had been: he stays in his room because he is afraid he will catch a cold or other infection out of doors (14:144), and he allows only necessary caretakers to come into his room, because he does not want to "let people see me and talk me over" (13:128).

COLIN'S PATHOLOGY

Burnett clearly indicates that Colin is a hypochondriac, a label her narrator uses later in the book (27:289). He once claimed to have a particular disease after having read about it (14:144), and Burnett's narrator says that "most of . . . [Colin's] fright and illness was created by himself" (17:181). After removing an iron brace the local doctor had put on Colin's back, a London doctor had said that there had "been too much medicine and too much lettin' him have his own way"; he prescribed fresh air and declared that Colin "might live if he would make up his mind to it" (8:129, 14:143, 149). This diagnosis of Colin's illness and prescription for curing it reflect Burnett's appreciative contact with the ideas of Mary Baker Eddy, who had founded

Christian Science in the late nineteenth century. In her depiction of how Colin's familial situation shaped Colin's illness, however, with its implicit testimony to the power of unconscious motivation, Burnett anticipates psychoanalytic theories that were not common currency until later in the twentieth century. Sigmund Freud was just beginning to publish his theories, in German, during the decade when Burnett was writing *The Secret Garden*.

Through his illness, it can be argued, Colin unconsciously lives out a perverse combination of his father's fears and wishes. When his wife died shortly after giving birth to Colin, Mr. Craven's excessive grief had almost institutionalized him. He had refused to see the baby, "raved" that it would inherit his own "hunchback," and declared that "it'd better die" (14:142). In all probability, the father never articulated these sentiments to his son; such messages, however, are often communicated indirectly. Once, when he had had typhoid, Colin overheard Mrs. Medlock express a fear he would die, adding that it would be the "best thing for him an' for everybody" (14:143). With the assistance of such overheard comments, Colin draws logical conclusions from his father's avoiding him. As he tells Mary, "My mother died when I was born and it makes him wretched to look at me. He thinks I don't know, but I've heard people talking. He almost hates me" (13:129). Later, he adds that he thinks his father wishes he would die (14:149). Mr. Craven's fears and wishes provide shape as well as motivation for his son's illness; Colin waits in terror for the lump on his back which will indicate that his hunchback has begun to grow and that he will soon die (15:164, 16:176, 17:180).

Just as Mary's autistic tendencies shortly after her parents' death had suggested an adaptive desire to take care of herself, Colin's illness serves a variety of similarly contradictory, unconscious purposes. On the one hand, the illness expresses Colin's desire to be loved. By living out his father's fears and wishes, Colin can please him and be like him. Colin knows that his father's crooked back had begun to show when he was a child (16:176). On the other hand, the illness expresses a fierce anger suicidally directed against himself. With his own illness and premature death, Colin can take revenge against his father for neglecting him. He can also punish himself for any responsibility he may feel for causing his mother's death. Jerry Griswold, in fact, suggests that Colin has an Oedipal guilt for having come between his parents.[1] It is likely true, as has often been suggested, that in her depiction of Colin, Burnett used her observations of her son Lionel's invalidism before his death at age 16 of tuberculosis; in addition, however, anger and probably guilt played a significant role in the psychosomatic illnesses she herself suffered, especially during difficult times in her relationships with her husbands.

A RAJAH'S CONTROL

Colin's most conscious anger is directed not at his father, however, but at his mother, who, because she is dead, provides a safer target. Most of the time Colin keeps a curtain closed over her portrait in his room, explaining to Mary that he blames her for all of his father's and his own troubles. "I don't see why she died. Sometimes I hate her for doing it," he says. "If she had lived I believe I should not have been ill always. . . . I dare say I should have lived, too. And my father would not have hated to look at me. I dare say I should have had a strong back. Draw the curtain again." The curtain obviously allows him to take revenge on his mother by putting her under his control. It also allows him to control others; "she is mine and I don't want everyone to see her," he adds to Mary (13:137).

Colin controls others through his illness as well. Because they fear that he might die during one of his temper tantrums or "hysterics" (18:177), his caretakers usually give him his way. And Colin's manipulation is deliberate according to Martha, who says that "when he's in a passion he'll fair scream just to frighten us. He knows us daren't call our souls our own" (14:141). In this way, too, Colin is like Mary who, "when she had had a headache in India . . . had done her best to see that everybody else also had a headache or something quite as bad" (16:170). Also like Mary in India, Colin has been educated to expect the privileges of a ruling class. This connection to Mary's own past is stressed when Mary compares Colin to a "boy" "Rajah" she once saw in India, who "spoke to his people just as you spoke to Martha. Everybody had to do everything he told them—in a minute" (14:146).

RETRACING MARY'S JOURNEY FORWARD

In her portrayal of Colin's journey from isolation and illness to friendship and health, Burnett shows him recapitulating much of the journey Mary has undergone so far, and Mary often plays a role in his journey similar to that which Martha and Ben had played in hers. Just as Martha had told Mary about the secret garden during her first morning at Misselthwaite, for example, Mary tells Colin about it during their first encounter at night. And Colin is immediately interested in the garden for some of the same reasons Mary had been. "Much like herself," Mary recognizes, Colin "too had had nothing to think about and the idea of a hidden garden attracted him as it had attracted her" (13:132). That the garden is "hidden" or secret represents one of its chief appeals for both children. Colin tells Mary he has never had a secret, except that he has hidden from his caretakers his belief that he will not live to grow up (13:135). Colin is ambivalent about this secret. When Mary asks, "Do you want to live?" he says "No," then quickly adds, "But I don't want to die." Learning about a hopeful secret, the garden, however, helps tip the balance away from death and toward life. "I like this kind [of secret] better," he tells Mary (13:133, 135).

THE POWER OF SECRECY

As Gillian Adams has pointed out, healing in this book often means trading bad secrets for good ones as well as learning the difference between good and bad kinds of control, and keeping a secret can be seen as a form of control.[2] These issues surface frequently during Mary's first discussion of the garden with Colin. Upon hearing about the garden and thinking "that the whole world belonged to him," Colin immediately decides to order his servants to take him there.

Mary manages to intercept that first impulse, however, by implying that keeping the garden secret would offer a more satisfying kind of control. "If no one knows but ourselves," she says, "we could find [the door] . . . and shut it behind us" so that "no one knew any one was inside" (13:132, 134).

In a secret garden, as Mary has already experienced, willful dependence on others can be replaced by independent power. She tells Colin that it would be "our garden," a place to play "almost every day" and "make it all come alive" (13:132, 134). Taking charge of the garden means beginning to take control of one's own life. Like Mary earlier, Colin has every reason to see the garden as another self: he, too, has been virtually locked up and forgotten by his father. This point is made when Mary first introduces the garden into their conversation. After Colin declares that his father "almost hates me," Mary says that "he hates the garden, because she died" (13:129).

The garden's connection to Colin's mother, of course, provides one of its greatest holds on his imagination. Mary tells him that it had been especially liked by her, that it had been when she died and Colin was born that his father had locked the garden and buried the key (13:129, 131). Even as Colin has never been told about the garden, he has apparently been kept mostly in the dark about his mother's life and death and his own birth. The secret garden thus offers a tantalizing key to these secret mysteries that have been such powerful determinants in his life. If he is to move forward, Colin desperately needs to form a more positive attitude toward his dead mother. He must get over the fear of "rose cold," which keeps him indoors (14:144); he must keep open the "rose-coloured silk curtain" that covers his mother's portrait in his room and tend the roses that are the dominant flowers in her garden (13:136, 135).

THERAPIST MARY

Colin recapitulates Mary's journey forward in many ways in addition to finding that the garden offers something new and hopeful to think about. In his interactions with Mary, he learns some of the lessons Mary had earlier learned with Martha. Already during their first visit, he begins a reciprocal relationship with her, sharing his mother's portrait after Mary divulges her knowledge about a secret garden. And Mary's description of Dickon's ability to charm animals overcomes Colin's class snobbishness as Martha's descriptions had earlier overcome Mary's.

Similarly, Colin's interactions with Mary reenact hers with the robin and Ben Weatherstaff. When Ben had told her that the robin was lonely, Mary had recognized that she was lonely, too. Now, after Mary tells Colin that Dickon can understand creatures because he is their friend, Colin says, "I never had anything to be friends with, and I can't bear people." Mary responds by recounting what Ben had told her about their both having "nasty tempers" and being "as sour as we looked": "We are all three alike," she declares. Following the example of therapist Ben earlier, Mary helps Colin understand his feelings by inviting him to project them onto herself. "Did you feel as if you hated people?" Colin asks. "Yes," Mary responds. "I should have detested you if I had seen you before I saw the robin and Dickon." As Mary had been surprised to find herself liking the robin and Ben, Colin tells Mary, "It's very funny, but I . . . like you" (18:191).

GIVING UP BAD KINDS OF SECRETS AND CONTROL

Colin's changes do not occur effortlessly; he does not easily give up his rajah-like desire to control others. At first he wants to control Mary by having her come when he dispatches Martha to fetch her and by keeping these visits secret from the rest of the household. When Mary chooses one morning to join Dickon in the garden rather than visit him, Colin throws a tantrum. Mary subsequently fights with him about Dickon, whom competitive Colin now calls a "common cottage boy off the moor," and she storms out of his room, saying she will not come back (16:172–73). It takes another tantrum before Colin is willing to give up his rajah-like treatment of Mary, a change precipitated by his revealing his secret fear and having it shown to be in error. In the presence of his nurse and Mrs. Medlock, Colin tells Mary that he has found a lump on his back which means he will soon die. After Mary examines him and discovers none, he asks his nurse, in a tone "not like a Rajah at all," if he could "live to grow up." She answers by quoting the London doctor: "You probably will if you do what you are told to do, and not give way to your temper, and stay out a great deal in the fresh air" (17:182).

These encounters between Mary and Colin contain some of the best portrayals of children fighting in children's literature—they are usually among the most effective scenes in film adaptations of the book. Burnett's earlier adaptations of her novels for the stage had taught her how to create dramatic conflict, and, as has already been asserted, in *The Secret Garden* her understanding of child motivation and behavior was fully engaged.

"WICKED" MARY

Because as a child she need not feel responsible for Colin's welfare, Mary succeeds with him where adults had failed. Through the vivid expression of Martha's and Dickon's mother, Mrs. Sowerby, Burnett suggests that children often learn best from other children that the whole world is not theirs to control. Mrs. Sowerby says, "When I was at school my jography told as th' world was shaped like a orange an' I found out before I was ten that th' whole orange doesn't belong to nobody. No one owns more than his bit of a quarter an' there's times it seems like there's not enow quarters to go round. . . . What children learns from children . . . is that there's no sense in grabbin' at th' whole orange—peel an' all. If you do you'll likely not get even th' pips, an' them's too bitter to eat" (19:198–99).

Being still "quite contrary" herself, child Mary is well suited to teaching Colin that he cannot have the "whole orange." It had been precisely because she was "rebellious" and "bold," for example, that she had managed to locate him in the first place: "I don't care about Mrs. Medlock—I don't care!" she had said as she began her candle-lit journey through the corridors (13:125).

Mary succeeds also because, like Colin, she, too, had once thought she could have the "whole orange." During their first visit, Burnett's narrator says, "Mary had not known that she herself had been spoiled, but she could see quite plainly that this mysterious boy had been" (13:132). Whether consciously acknowledged or not, this resemblance allows her to recognize Colin's manipulative tactics and call his bluff. Having once given everyone else a headache because she had one, she is now not sympathetic when Colin talks about dying. "I don't believe it!" she tells him. "You just say that to make people sorry. I believe you're proud of it" (16:170, 173). And when he wakens her during the night with one of his tantrums—thrown because she will not let him control her visits to Dickon—Mary gets so "angry" she feels "as if she should like to fly into a tantrum herself." When "wicked," "savage" Mary reaches Colin's room, she tells him, "You stop! I hate you! Everybody hates you! I wish everybody would run out of the house and let you scream yourself to death!" "There's nothing the matter with your horrid back—nothing but hysterics!" she adds. "Turn over and let me look at it!" (17:17–80).

Nurturant Mary

Mary is not always "wicked" and "savage" in her dealings with Colin; at times she is more sympathetic. As she enjoys hurling the adult word *hysterics* at him when she is angry, she also sometimes adopts the adult role of his nurse. At the conclusion of their first visit, at night, she feels "somehow . . . sorry for him" and does "not want him to lie awake," and so she strokes his hand while singing a Hindustani song, as her Ayah had done for her in India (13:138). And, after the nighttime visit that reveals that Colin has no lump on his back, Mary tells the "yawning nurse," "I will put him to sleep. . . . You can go if you like." This time, however, Mary accedes to Colin's request that instead of singing a Hindustani song she "softly" describe what she imagines the secret garden might look like—not until the next day does Mary trust him with the secret that she has already been inside (17:183–85, 18:193).

Because the ability to nurture others was a significant part of how adult female roles were defined when Burnett wrote *The Secret Garden*, Mary's becoming a nurse to Colin signals that she is beginning to grow up. In addition, as is already obvious, the effects of appropriate nurturance or its lack is one of Burnett's primary preoccupations in this book. Her mythic enlargement of this theme is evident in Mary's description of the secret garden to make Colin relax so that he can sleep: "I think the ground is full of daffodils and snowdrops and lilies and iris working their way out of the dark. Now the spring has begun—perhaps . . . they are coming up through the grass—perhaps there are clusters of purple crocuses and gold ones—even now" (17:184–85). With its emphasis on springtime changes, Mary's description of the garden links the crucial change Colin has just undergone, as well as Mary's own earlier change, with the rebirthing power of nature.

7

Nest Building (Chapters 13–20)

The transformation of Mary and Colin is linked with the powers of nature not only through the seasonal cycle but also through a chain of nest imagery. For example, the secret garden is several times identified as Mary's "nest." In an earlier chapter, when Mary had asked Dickon to keep her garden a secret, he had replied, "If tha' was a missel thrush an' showed me where thy nest was, does tha' think I'd tell any one?" Later, in the garden, he had left Mary his drawing of a bird on its nest with the message "I will cum back" (12:123), which Mary interprets to mean that "her garden was her nest and she was like a missel thrush" (12:123, 13:124). In her secret garden or nest, orphan Mary has found the nurturant home she has long needed, and she soon recognizes that motherless Colin would find it similarly appealing. Her attempt to keep Colin from telling anyone about the garden includes the suggestion that they could pretend "that we were missel thrushes and and it was our nest" (13:134).

Nest Building *(Chapters 13–20)*

NESTS AND NURTURANCE

The role of the secret garden as a nest is further enhanced by the fact that it had been a favorite of Colin's mother. Gardens and nests were common metaphors for homes and female nurturance at the time Burnett wrote *The Secret Garden*. They can be found also, for example, in Kate Douglas Wiggin's *Mother Carey's Chickens*, published the same year Burnett's classic appeared as a book. The connection between the garden and a mother's nurturance is made by some of Mary's actions and Dickon's response. Earlier, Ben had told Mary that Mrs. Craven had loved the garden's flowers "like they was children— or robins. I've seen her bend over an' kiss 'em" (10:94). Now, in the garden with Dickon, Mary similarly kisses the flowers. When she observes, however, that "you never kiss a person in that way," Dickon replies, "I've kissed mother many a time that way when I come in from th' moor after a day's roamin' and she stood there at th' door in th' sun, lookin' so glad an' comfortable" (15:160–61). Later, Mrs. Sowerby, like Mary and Mrs. Craven, will stoop over the flowers and talk about them as if they were children (26:284).

Mary and Dickon soon recognize that Colin would benefit by joining them in this comfortable nest. "It'd be good for him," Dickon says. "Us'd not be thinkin' he'd better never been born. Us'd be just two children watchin' a garden grow, an' he'd be another" (15:166). As should be obvious by now, images in *The Secret Garden* often have several possible meanings. The garden can be seen as a nest where the children are nurturers as well as nurtured. Mary in the garden can be seen as not only a baby bird but also a mother bird, as is suggested by the description of Dickon's drawing as "a nest with a bird sitting on [not *in*] it " (12:123).

Nest-building as part of mating is stressed during Mary's second exploration of the garden with Dickon. The robin, who had earlier been portrayed in his cocky search for a mate, is now "settin' up housekeepin' " (15:162), and Mary and Dickon can be seen as engaging in this activity, too. In addition to their parental plans to bring Colin to the garden, they already have two other children to play with, a fox cub and crow Dickon has brought with him (15:159–60).

And sometime later, Dickon brings a newborn lamb, which Mary, "full of strange joy," holds in her "lap like a baby" (19:201). That Colin is another baby animal for them to nurture is suggested by parallel descriptions of how the lamb and Colin are found. Just as Mary had found Colin by following his cry through rooms and corridors, Dickon had heard the lamb bleating on the moors and had taken a similarly tortuous route to find it: "I went in an' out among th' gorse bushes an' round an' round an' I always seemed to take th' wrong turnin'. But at last I seed a bit o' white by a rock on top o' th' moor an' I climbed up an' found th' little 'un half dead w' cold and clemmin' [starving]" (19:205).

NESTS AND MATING

The suggestion that Mary and Dickon are nurturant parents of Colin is congruent with the latent sexuality of their first exploration of the garden. In their subsequent visits, too, their mutual discovery of the garden is portrayed as a rich feast for the senses. The observation that Mary "kissed and kissed" the flowers is soon followed by "they put their eager young noses close to the earth and sniffed its warmed springtime breathing; they dug and pulled and laughed low with rapture until Mistress Mary's hair was as tumbled as Dickon's and her cheeks were almost as poppy red as his" (15:161). The chapter ends as Dickon and Mary are watching the robin and his mate build a nest for their future babies, and Dickon's comment to the robins suggests that he and Mary are co-conspirators sharing similar secrets: "Tha' knows us won't trouble thee. . . . Us is nest-buildin' too, bless thee. Look out tha' doesn't tell on us" (15:167).

In this passage Burnett may have been drawing, however unconsciously, on the the idea of a garden as site for surreptitious trysts, an idea at least as old as the thirteenth-century *Romance of the Rose*. Through her portrayal of the garden as a special retreat for Mr. and Mrs. Craven before her death, Burnett follows the modern tradition, articulated in Jean-Jacques Rousseau's *New Eloise* (1761), of having the garden symbolize marital bliss rather than illicit passion. The association of the garden with romantic love was made in the 1980 television movie. In this adaptation Mary and Colin have no family relationship, and the movie ends when, as young adults, they are betrothed in the garden.

If the sexual connotations of secret gardens are suggested by Mary's enjoyment of the garden with Dickon, they can be found also in the description of the garden she uses to relax Colin so he can sleep after his last tantrum. Ostensibly a lullaby, it can also be read as a seductive invitation, for Mary's description of the changes spring is bringing to the garden sometimes seems like a celebration of the female genital being transformed during puberty. "It has grown all into a lovely tangle. I think the roses have climbed and climbed and climbed until they hang from the branches and walls and creep over the ground—almost like a strange grey mist"; "the grey is changing and a green gauze veil is creeping—and creeping over—everything. And the birds are coming to look at it—because it is—so safe and still." Suggesting the resemblance between a mature female genital and a nest, this passage is immediately followed by the possibility that "perhaps . . . the robin has found a mate—and is building a nest" (18:184–85).

COLIN AND DICKON AS OPPOSITES

Colin responds to this description not as Mary's potential lover, however, but as her soothed child; he falls asleep. This action dramatizes the very different roles Colin and wide-awake Dickon are playing in Mary's life. The boys are in many ways polar opposites. While Dickon spends his days moving about outside on the moors, Colin remains immobilized within his shut-up and thus relatively dark room. While Dickon is so much attuned to his body and its delights that he sometimes seems more animal than human, Colin's body has virtually atrophied from lack of use—he can barely sit unassisted let alone walk. While Burnett's descriptions of Dickon's face had noted his "big mouth," suggesting his healthy bodily appetite, her initial descriptions of Colin emphasize his head, and especially those windows to the interior of the head, his eyes, which are a stony "agate grey" compared to

Dickon's eyes of sky blue (12:114–15, 13:127). Over and over, Burnett tells us that Colin's eyes are "immense," "too big" for his "sharp, delicate face the colour of ivory" (13:126–27). Once Colin's eyes are described as "big as the wolf's in Red Riding Hood" (20:215)—a significant avoidance of the more memorable teeth of the wolf, an animal that in this and other stories is known for its prodigious appetite.

A study in contrasts, Dickon and Colin often confront Mary with competing loyalties. She begins to compare the two soon after she meets Colin. Being told, the morning after their first visit, that Colin wants to see her, Mary considers that "she did not want to see Colin as much as she wanted to see Dickon," and when she tells Colin he reminds her of a rajah, she adds that he is very "different" from Dickon (14:145–46). Colin is clearly cognizant of this competition; Mary's subsequent decision to join Dickon in the garden rather than visit him in his room precipitates a day-long sulk and the threat that "I won't let that boy come here if you go and stay with him instead of coming to talk with me" (16:171). The 1993 movie, which in a number of ways makes more explicit the text's sexual undertones, hints that the children form a romantic triangle. In a garden scene, Colin is visibly upset when Mary and Dickon enjoy an intense, extended gaze while sharing a swing.

A FAMILIAR TRIANGLE

A heroine who divides her attention between an eroticized lower-class male and an attenuated upper-class male has occurred elsewhere in British fiction. An earlier example of this character triad had been provided by Catherine, Heathcliff, and Edgar, who, along with their Yorkshire moors in Emily Brontë's *Wuthering Heights* (1847), doubtless influenced Burnett consciously or unconsciously in writing *The Secret Garden*. A similar trio has caused Kathleen Verduin and Judith Plotz to suggest that Burnett's book was an unacknowledged, possibly unconscious source for D. H. Lawrence's *Lady Chatterley's Lover* (1928). The many similarities Verduin and Plotz identify between

Nest Building (Chapters 13–20)

Mary Lennox and Connie Chatterley, Dickon Sowerby and Oliver Mellors, and Colin Craven and Clifford Chatterley are indeed striking. Both books connect verdurous nature with human sexuality, the once notorious details of Connie's love affair with gardener Mellors bringing to the surface the latent sexuality of Mary's discovery of the garden with Dickon. Both books see a "return to the full life of the body as healing," as Plotz notes.[1] Unlike Lawrence, however, Burnett extends this healing to the landed aristocracy, as represented by Colin and his father. This hopeful attitude derives not only from Burnett's different attitude toward class but also from the fact that she was in part writing a fairy tale, a kind of story characterized by magic transformations.

MAGIC TRANSFORMATIONS

In the chapters depicting the children's plans to bring Colin to the garden, it becomes apparent that Burnett is using "Magic" as a unifying metaphor for the various kinds of transformations in her book. The changes spring brings to the garden are magic: "The garden had reached the time when every day and every night it seemed as if Magicians were passing through it drawing loveliness out of the earth and the boughs with wands" (18:189). And the changes within the children are similarly magic. To describe their amazement at Mary's ability to calm Colin, Martha and Mrs. Medlock both declare that she has "bewitched" him (14:142, 19:194). Dickon has a similar effect on Colin, and Burnett's narrator claims that there "really" is "a sort of Magic about Dickon as Mary always privately believed" (20:209). Mary tells Colin that with his pipe Dickon "can charm foxes and squirrels and birds just as the natives in India charm snakes" (14:147), and Colin decides he would not mind a visit from Dickon because "he's a sort of animal charmer and I am a boy animal" (15:157).

Colin's recognition that he is a "boy animal" points the direction toward his healing. Even before he enters the garden, he shows that he will allow it to awaken his bodily senses. When Mary comes in from the garden and sits by his bed, he begins "to sniff as Dickon did, though not in such an experienced way." "You smell like flowers and—and fresh things," he "joyously" cries out. "What is it you smell of? It's cool and warm and sweet all at the same time" (18:189). During a later visit when he smells that she has been outside, he asks her to open his window so that the formerly feared fresh air can come inside (19:200). Colin welcomes the outside into his room also in the person of Dickon and his animals, some of which go in and out the open window as the children converse.

Dickon's animals initiate Colin into the joys of being nurturant—joys that Mary and Dickon had earlier discovered. When Dickon places the newborn lamb in Colin's lap, it nuzzles into the folds of his dressing gown because, as Dickon explains, "It wants its mother," and Colin holds it while Dickon feeds it with a bottle (19:204–205). Immediately following this action is Dickon's description of finding the lamb, which implicitly compares the lamb to Colin. Colin's nursing the lamb can thus suggest that he is beginning to take responsibility for meeting his own needs even as Mary's earlier work in the garden had indicated her ability to nurture herself.

MAGIC LANGUAGE

Transformations in fairy tales are often effected by magic words, and in Burnett's tale, too, language often seems to have a preternatural power. There are repeated tributes to the descriptive power of language. When Mary tells Colin about the beauty of the moor during the daytime, he is surprised to learn that she has not seen it but only heard about it from Martha and Dickon. "When Dickon talks about it," Mary says, "you feel as if you saw things and heard them, and as if you were standing in the heather with the sun shining and the gorse smelling like honey—and all full of bees and butterflies" (14:148). As language can transport you to another place, it can also bring a person not present closer to you. Earlier in this scene, Mary had "longed to talk about" Dickon because "it would seem to bring him nearer" (14:146). This power to control others is a traditional use of magic language in fairy tales, another good example being when Mary's description of the garden puts Colin to sleep and provides the landscape of his dreams. "I dreamed about it all night," Colin tells her the next morning. "I heard you say something about grey changing into green, and I dreamed I was standing in a place all filled with trembling little green leaves" (18:187).

In fairy tales magic words such as "Open Sesame" can sometimes affect nature itself. With their incantatory lists of changes brought to the moor and the garden, some speeches by Martha, Ben, and Dickon seem as much conjuring invocations as descriptions of spring. Early in the novel, for example, Martha tells Mary, "Just you wait till you see th' gold-coloured gorse blossoms an' th' blossoms o' th' broom, an' th' heather flowerin', all purple bells, an' hundreds o' butterflies flutterin' an' bees hummin' an skylarks soarin' up an' singin'" (7:61). Later Dickon introduces his own list of transformations with the idea, implicit in some religious rituals, that in each individual new beginning we participate in our collective original beginning: "Th' world's all fair begun again this mornin', it has. An it's workin' an' hummin' an' scratchin' an' pipin' an' nest-buildin' an' breathin' out scents, till you've got to be out on it 'stead o' lyin' on your back" (15:159–60).

No doubt it is partly because Mary believes that there is "a sort of Magic about Dickon" that she tries to learn his language. The power of his Yorkshire dialect is suggested by the fact that Mary's first long speech in that dialect describes plans to help Colin change by having him meet Dickon and witness for himself springtime's changes in the garden. Colin has taken "a graidely fancy to thee," Mary says to Dickon. "I'll ax him if tha' canna come an' see him tomorrow mornin'—an' bring tha' creatures wi' thee—an' then—in a bit, when there's more leaves out, an' happen a bud or two, we'll get him to come out an' tha' shall push him in his chair an' we'll bring him here an' show him everything." That the Yorkshire dialect can have medicinal power over Colin is suggested by Dickon's response: "Tha' mun talk a bit o' Yorkshire like that to Mester Colin. . . . Tha'll make him laugh an' there's nowt as good for ill folk as laughin' is. Mother says she believes as half a hour's good laugh every mornin' 'ud cure a chap as was making ready for typhus fever" (18:188–89).

MAGIC RITUALS

Magic ritual as well as magic language plays a role in the children's celebration of the transformations they are experiencing in nature and
within themselves. Journeys associated with these changes are often
perceived to be processions. When Mary rushes into Colin's room to
announce "It is here now! It has come, the Spring!" Colin responds,
"Open the window. . . . Perhaps we may hear golden trumpets!"
(19:200). Later Colin tells Mary that her announcement of spring had
"sounded as if things were coming with a great procession and big
bursts and wafts of music." The procession he imagines was inspired
by a picture in one of his books, a picture of "crowds of lovely people
and children with garlands and branches with blossoms on them, every
one laughing and dancing and crowding and playing on pipes." "That
was why I said, 'Perhaps we shall hear golden trumpets' and told you
to throw open the window," he adds. "That's really just what it feels
like," Mary agrees, and she embellishes his picture by adding nonhuman revelers to the procession: "And if all the flowers and leaves and
green things and birds, and wild creatures danced past at once, what a
crowd it would be!" (20:212–13).

The children do not simply imagine processions; they experience
them. The first appearance of Dickon and his creatures in the manor is
described as a processional march. Before Dickon reaches Colin's
room, Mary and Colin hear the caw of his crow, the bleat of his lamb,
and the "clumping sound" of his "moorland boots" "marching—
marching" (19:203). And the long-awaited and carefully planned first
journey the three children make to the secret garden is similarly ritual-
istic. Ritual often involves reenactment, as when religious devotees
mystically partake in the power of an earlier event—such as Christ's
death and resurrection—by a reenactment of some aspect of it—such
as the Mass. Somewhat similarly, Colin's first journey to the secret garden reenacts Mary's earlier journey, as if to assure that her healing in
the garden will be experienced by Colin as well. As Dickon pushes
Colin in his chair, Mary points out where she used "to walk up and
down and wonder and wonder." She points out "where Ben
Weatherstaff works," "where the robin flew over the wall," "where he

perched on the little heap of earth and showed me the key," and where the wind blew back the ivy so that she could see the hidden door (20:214–15).

The ritualistic nature of this scene is underscored by the repetitive, antiphonal nature of the children's dialogue. Three times after Mary points to a place where something important earlier occurred, Colin says "Is it?" and a fourth time he says "Oh! is it—is it!" That Colin is ritually recapitulating earlier discoveries of the garden is suggested also when, once inside the garden, he looks "round and round and round as Dickon and Mary had done" (20:214–16). Finally, to express the new hope he receives from the garden, Colin uses words first phrased by Dickon and then repeated by Mary to Colin, "I shall live forever and ever and ever!" (19:200, 20:216).

8

Parental Reunions (Chapters 21–27)

The repetition with variation that characterizes the children's ritual-istic action and language in the garden also provides the structure for Burnett's book. Already noted have been ways in which Colin's jour-ney to health repeats Mary's, and the parallel nature of these two journeys is underscored by the amount of attention Burnett pays to each. She uses eight chapters (1–8) to establish Mary's character and get her inside the secret garden and another eight (13–20) to intro-duce Colin and bring him to the garden. Moreover, each group of eight chapters is followed by a similarly parallel group of four (9–12 and 21–24) depicting first Mary's and then Colin's transformations within the garden. The book's final three chapters (25–27) can be seen as a coda that recapitulates this theme through an abbreviated depiction of Mr. Craven's transformation and at the same time pulls together various earlier patterns of imagery, especially those related to parental nurturance.

FILLING A PARENTAL VACUUM

Developing a more positive attitude toward both of his parents plays an essential part of Colin's journey to physical and psychological health during the final chapters of *The Secret Garden*. As has been suggested earlier, much of Colin's pathology has resulted from his feeling abandoned by his mother and rejected by his father. This lack of parental affirmation has virtually infantilized him, making him both tyrannically egocentric and incapable of caring for himself. As has also been suggested, Mary and Dickon instinctively try to fill this parental vacuum by plotting to bring Colin to the garden and, once inside, by treating him with nurturant solicitude. They set him under a tree and bring him things to look at; they wheel him around to show him the garden's riches; and they are particularly protective of his presumed psychological fragility. They have previously discussed what they will do if Colin asks about the dead tree with the branch which broke when Colin's mother sat on it just before her death. "We couldn't never tell him how it broke, poor lad," Dickon had said. When Colin does in fact ask about the branch, Dickon diverts his attention to the robin foraging for his mate, and Mary considers the robin's appearance at this moment a fortuitous example of "Magic" (21:221). Indulgence and overprotection, however, are not what Colin needs for continuing recovery; it is now time that he confront rather than avoid his mother's death and his father's rejection. This confrontation occurs through his interactions with two who as adults can more easily reflect his feelings about his parents, the gardener Ben Weatherstaff and Dickon's mother, Susan Sowerby.

BEN WEATHERSTAFF AS SURROGATE FATHER

During Colin's first visit to the garden he sees Ben Weatherstaff peering over the wall from a ladder on the opposite side. When Colin asks if Ben knows who he is, the gardener replies by articulating the view of Colin that the boy knows helped cause his father's rejection of him: "tha'rt th' poor cripple" (21:226). Shortly before this interchange with

Ben, Dickon had predicted that when Colin loses his fear he will be able to stand and walk. Anger, however, proves to be the provocation he needs. "His anger and insulted pride" at Ben's description of him as a "cripple" fill "him with a power he had never known before, an almost unnatural strength." Leaning on Dickon's arm, he stands upright "as straight as an arrow . . . his strange eyes flashing lightning"; with Dickon's assistance, he walks to a tree and supports himself against it (21:227–28, 22:231). Colin's anger impels him not only to stand and walk but also to assert his authority over gardener Ben. "I'm your master . . . when my father is away. And you are to obey me." And Colin continues this imperious attitude toward Ben despite the old gardener's repeated apologies and litanies of "Yes, sir!" (21:228–29).

In part, Colin's treatment of Ben reflects his class consciousness; its vehemence, however, may result from the fact that Ben has articulated the vision of himself held by many others, including especially his own father. By striking out at Ben, the boy is in part venting his anger at his father, as well as exorcizing the self-image he himself has carried for so long. This is not the first time Ben has provided a therapist-like screen for a child's projections, as was pointed out earlier in discussion of his interactions with Mary. And, as earlier, Ben ultimately affirms the child's healthier impulses. Observing the upright Colin, Ben declares that the reports he heard about Colin were "lies," and he gives Colin the approbation that the boy would so like to receive from his father: "Tha'lt make a mon yet. God bless thee!" (21:228).

Subsequent comments by Colin indicate how much of his recovery is motivated by a desire to prove to his father that his estimate of his son is wrong. He insists that no one tell his father so that he can deliver this news in person, and he creates imaginary scenarios about how he will confront his father with his healthy self. "The thought which stimulated him more than any other," we are told, "was . . . imagining what his father would look like when he saw that he had a son who was as straight and strong as other father's [*sic*] sons." "One of his darkest miseries in the unhealthy morbid past days," Burnett's narrator says, "had been his hatred of being a sickly weak-backed boy whose father was afraid to look at him" (23:249–50). When his doctor suggests telling his father that he seems to be improving, Colin responds as "fiercely" as earlier to Ben (24:258). "I want to tell him myself," he later tells Mary, adding, "I'm always thinking about it," which suggests that proving himself to his father has become something of a fixed idea (25:271).

A MOTHER'S CONTINUING CARE

If the completion of Colin's recovery is dependent on his angry determination to prove his father wrong about him, he must also change his attitude toward his mother's effect on his life. During their first confrontation in the garden, Ben Weatherstaff sets him in the right direction on this matter as well. When Colin asks him if he knows who he is, Ben says, "Aye, that I do—wi' tha' mother's eyes starin' at me out o' tha' face" (21:226). Earlier, Dickon had reported to Mary that Colin's father "can't bear to see him when he's awake . . . because his eyes is so like his mother's" (15:164). Though we are never told that Colin has heard this reported connection between his resemblance to his mother and his father's rejection, he might well have deduced it. During his first conversation with Mary, he had twice attributed a causal relationship between his mother's death and his father's hating to look at him, once immediately before Mary told him that his mother's eyes, in her portrait, are "just like" his (13:129, 137).

If Colin is to regard his resemblance to his mother as an asset rather than a liability, he must form an image of her that goes beyond the single fact of her death. Once again, Ben Weatherstaff offers him crucial information during their first encounter in the garden. Colin learns that Ben was especially liked by his mother and continues to be employed in the estate gardens "because she liked me." Moreover, Colin learns that Ben had "come over the wall" to tend the secret garden because she had told him to care for her roses if she could no longer do so. For eight years, until rheumatism prevented him, Ben had defied Colin's father's prohibition of the garden to everyone, because Colin's mother had given "her order first" (12:232–34). Ben's divulgences encourage Colin to see his mother not as someone who abandoned him but as someone whose caring continues in the present, through her favored gardener as well as the garden itself. Already bringing him health and making him feel he will live "forever and ever" (20:216), the garden is his inheritance from his mother, one he is now ready to claim. "This was her garden, wasn't it?" Colin asks Ben. When Ben agrees, Colin asserts, "It is my garden now" (22:233).

By the last three chapters or "coda" to *The Secret Garden*, Colin's recovery in the garden has been completed, and he is ready for a psychological and spiritual reunion with his mother as well as a more physical one with his father. In chapter 25, after a rainy-day exploration of the manor, Mary notices that the curtain that once covered his mother's portrait is now open. Colin explains that his mother's laughing face no longer makes him angry, because he now interprets her laughter not as a derisive commentary on his own unhappiness (13:137) but as an affirmation of his new health. "She looked right down at me as if she were laughing because she was glad I was standing there," Colin says. With this maternal affirmation, he can be more hopeful about how his father will now react to his resemblance to her. When Mary observes, "You are so like her now . . . that sometimes I think perhaps you are her ghost made into a boy," Colin asserts, "If I were her ghost—my father would be fond of me" (25:274–75).

SUSAN SOWERBY AS SURROGATE MOTHER

In the next chapter, Susan Sowerby, mother of Dickon and Martha, provides Colin another affirmation of his mother's love and his father's probable appreciation of his resemblance to her. As Colin, Mary, Dickon, and Ben are celebrating nature's transformative "Magic" in the secret garden, Mrs. Sowerby makes her way through the garden door. Colin and Mary have never met her, but what they have heard has convinced them she could be told about their secret, and she has been sending them fresh milk and baked goods to eat in the garden so that their healthy appetites do not reveal Colin's recovery before his father comes home (24:256). With her ready laughter, basket of food, and invitation to visit her moor cottage with its 12 children, Mrs. Sowerby easily reflects Colin's maternal fantasies even as the initially stern but ultimately affirming Ben Weatherstaff had provided an apt stand-in for Colin's father. Like Ben, Mrs. Sowerby immediately comments on Colin's striking resemblance to his mother, and, when he asks, she assures the boy that this will indeed make his father like him (26:282). Equally important, this "comfortable wonderful mother creature" becomes a living conduit for his own mother's continuing love (24:257). When Colin says, "I wish you were my mother," she embraces him, saying, "Thy own mother's in this 'ere garden I do believe. She couldna' keep out of it" (26:287).

Mrs. Sowerby's assertion brings to the surface of Burnett's text a motif from the Cinderella tale that more obviously undergirded *Little Lord Fauntleroy*, *A Little Princess,* and some of Burnett's adult fiction. In some variants of the Cinderella tale, the magic that assists the heroine is associated with her dead mother. In the Grimms' version, which Burnett undoubtedly knew, Cinderella is assisted not by a fairy godmother but by birds who live in a tree growing out of her mother's grave. The idea that Colin's mother is somehow present in the garden that was the occasion for her death and is now helping her son get well is not dissimilar to this Cinderella tale motif. Indeed, there are several other indications that Colin's mother may be an important source of the transforming "Magic" at work in Burnett's book. Earlier, for example, Dickon had told Mary that his mother "thinks maybe" Mrs. Craven is "about Misselthwaite many a time lookin' after Mester Colin, same as all mothers do when they're took out o' th' world. They have to come back, tha' sees. Happen she's been in the garden an' happen it was her set us to work, an' told us to bring him here" (21:221). These assertions are what encouraged Marsha Norman to create a major role for Colin's mother as a protective ghost in her 1991 Broadway musical adaptation of *The Secret Garden*.

"A Sort of Magic Person"

Congruent with the Grimms' Cinderella tale, Colin's mother works her "Magic" through elements and creatures from nature, specifically wind, rain, moonlight, and the robin. It had been because a rushing wind opened the door to Mary's room and another door down the corridor that the girl first heard Colin's cry (5:50–51), and she had eventually found him one night after being awakened by the wind and rain during a springtime storm. Mary herself believes that the robin magically showed her where the garden key was buried and that "Magic" later sent a gust of wind to blow away the ivy to reveal the garden door (8:75–76). Colin, too, experiences his mother's magic through an element of nature. According to Colin, a "patch of moonlight on the curtain" one night made him "go and pull the cord" to open the curtain over his mother's portrait. The "bright moonlight" had made him feel that "the Magic was filling the room," he says, concluding that his mother "must have been a sort of Magic person" (25:274).

Careful reading of the book's last chapter shows that this "Magic person" and her garden help transform her husband as well as son. An early, though temporary, lifting of Mr. Craven's depression comes as he is resting by an alpine stream filled with "laughter as it bubbled over and round stones," recalling the laughter in his wife's portrait. A mass of forget-me-nots quiets him, and he begins to experience the "awakening" Mary and Colin had felt in the secret garden. Suggesting that there is indeed a kind of magic at work in Mr. Craven's recovery, we are told that this early awakening occurred on the very day Colin first entered the garden. As the seasons pass, Mr. Craven finds himself " 'coming alive' with the garden," just as are the children back home. With the coming of autumn—the season for harvesting summertime's growth—Mr. Craven wonders if he should go home and ponders what he will think when he looks again at his sleeping child (27:291–93).

He continues to shrink from this thought, however, until one night when the moonlight by a lake calms him into a deep sleep. Earlier, Burnett had described his depression as a darkness he had neurotically nursed, refusing "obstinately to allow any rift of light to pierce through" (27:290); now, however, the moonlight, which had earlier invited Colin to draw the curtains to reveal his mother's picture, manages to pierce Mr. Craven's depression as well. He breathes "the scent" of his wife's favorite "roses" and hears her calling his

name, telling him she is "in the garden." When he awakens, a servant
presents him with a letter inviting him to come home, written by the
woman who had spoken for his dead wife to Colin as well. "I think
your lady would ask you to come if she was here," Mrs. Sowerby
writes (27:294–95).

ARCHIBALD CRAVEN'S RECAPITULATIVE JOURNEY

As has been noted, Colin's recovery had repeated many features of
Mary's. Now Mr. Craven's journey to the garden recapitulates Mary's
and recalls some of Colin's earlier feelings. Like Mary earlier, Mr.
Craven is described taking the "long railroad journey" (27:296) across
the Yorkshire moors, uncertain about what lies ahead. Before going to
the manor to see his son, he stops to seek counsel from Mrs. Sowerby,
who had earlier advised him about Mary's rearing. Finding her not at
home, he solicits Mrs. Medlock's description of Colin in the library
before making his way to the garden, these delays suggesting that he is
as anxious about the coming reunion as Colin once was. And when
Burnett describes his eventual outdoor trip to the garden, she deliber-
ately asks the reader to recall Mary's earlier discovery of it. He walks,
"as Mary had done, through the door in the shrubbery and among the
the laurels and the fountain beds"; like Mary earlier, he notices the
"ivy hung thick" over the garden door and wonders if he can find the
buried key (27:300–301).

Burnett's description of what Mr. Craven discovers at the garden
door suggests that the wife who has magically called him back home is
waiting there to participate in the family reunion. The walled garden
that Mr. Craven had sealed up as if it were her tomb has now become
her womb, teaming with life and about to give birth. He hears "the
sounds of running, scuffling feet," "the uncontrollable laughter of children who were trying not to be heard but who in a moment or so—as
their excitement mounted—would burst forth" (27:301). Just as, two
chapters previously, the "rose-coloured" curtain (13:136) had been
opened to reveal the smiling face in his wife's portrait, the door of her
garden is now "flung wide open, the sheet of ivy swinging back." At

this "uncontrollable moment" Colin "burst[s] through it at full speed"; in an "unseeing dash" the boy earlier described by his doctor as "a new creature" now falls into his father's "extended" arms (27:301–302, 24:265). Soon after comes a healthy Mary, now part of this reunited family as well.

THE GARDEN AS SYMBOLIC CENTER

This suggestion of childbirth as the garden delivers its autumn harvest of health succinctly reminds the reader of all the garden has come to mean during the course of Burnett's novel. Being walled and locked, it had symbolized Mary's, Colin's, and Mr. Craven's psychological isolation; being neglected, it had resembled the orphaned Mary and virtually orphaned Colin; being apparently dead when rediscovered, it had been an image of the children's physical and psychological ills; having immediately preceded and perhaps precipitated Mrs. Craven's death, it had signaled the end of Mr. Craven's interest in his own or his son's life. Now, however, it has found gardeners who have helped it take best advantage of the changing seasons' transformative power, just as the children have received the kind of nurturance needed to free their healthier impulses; now, having divulged all of its secrets, the garden can complete its transformation of Mr. Craven as well. In this final chapter describing how Mr. Craven ritualistically reenacts the children's earlier journeys to the garden, Burnett calls attention to the garden's central role in all of her book's rebirths by repeating the phrase "in the garden" 12 times, beginning with Mrs. Craven's telling her husband, in his dream, that he could find her back home "in the garden" and ending with his own, astonished "In the garden! In the garden!" when confronted by a healthy Colin (27:294, 302).

THE SECRET GARDEN AS RELIGIOUS EXEMPLUM

Burnett's emphasis on rebirth indicates that she was influenced by not only the fairy tale but also another kind of story she had read as a

child, the exemplum. Deriving from the stories used in medieval ser-
mons to illustrate theological truths and divine imperatives, religious
exempla early in the nineteenth century had often featured a child
who is saved and then goes about saving others, often adults. Similarly,
The Secret Garden portrays Mary being "saved" and then helping to
"save" Colin; finally, the example of the children's "rebirths" helps
bring about Archibald Craven's.

To explain the power behind the "salvations" in her book,
Burnett draws from several literary and religious traditions. By using a
garden as the primary agent of rebirth and by idealizing the Yorkshire
rural folk—who presumably live more naturally and virtuously than
their aristocratic neighbors and masters—Burnett draws on a tradition
of literary pastoral at least as old as the poems about shepherds and
farmers written by the classical authors Theocritus and Virgil. The story
can also be seen as the loss and regaining of Eden in that the secret garden is initially fallen from and then restored to its former glory even as
Mary and Colin are initially far from being the innocents often portrayed in late-nineteenth-century children's literature, such as Burnett's
own *Little Lord Fauntleroy*. In addition, Burnett drew inspiration from
the pagan emphasis on an often matriarchal deity that is immanent in
nature as compared to the patriarchal, transcendent deity frequently
visaged in the Judeo-Christian tradition. The earlier comparison of
Dickon to the nature deity Pan is an obvious example of this pagan tradition, as is the presentation of Mrs. Sowerby as an earth mother.

These religious strands in Burnett's narrative find their fullest
expression in her last seven chapters. At the opening of chapter 21
Burnett's narrator joins the chorus of lyric rhapsodies to nature initiated
by Martha, Ben, Dickon, and Mary. The narrator observes that, like
Colin on first entering the garden, one sometimes feels immortal while
glimpsing what the Renaissance poet Edmund Spenser called the
"eterne in mutability" (*Faerie Queene,* III, vi, 4.5). "One is quite sure
one is going to live forever" when "one's heart stands still at the strange
unchanging majesty of the rising sun—which has been happening every
morning for thousands and thousands and thousands of years"
(21:217). Similarly, in chapter 23, Burnett describes the children's
delight as they watch the daily changes occurring in the garden, not

only in the growing plants and budding flowers but also in the behavior of its many creatures: "ants' ways, beetles' ways, bees' ways, frogs' ways, birds' ways" all provide "a new world to explore" (23:240–41). As before, the children use the word *Magic* to describe the power responsible for these changes, and Colin makes himself "High Priest" of this garden religion (23:247).

THE GARDEN RELIGION

Colin makes Dickon, Mary, and Ben stand in a row and listen to his sermon about how the magic making things grow in the garden is a power he can also use to make himself well (23:243–44). He has all of them, including Dickon's birds and animals, sit with him in a circle under a tree, which he says is "like sitting in a sort of temple" (23:246). He voices a "chant" celebrating the power of the magic, and he leads them in a "a procession . . . slowly but with dignity" around the garden (23:49). The religious nature of these activities is underscored by Ben's thinking that he has "somehow been led into appearing at a prayer-meeting" (23:246–47). A similar ceremony occurs in chapter 26. When Colin says he wants to "shout out" "something thankful, joyful" because he is now well, Ben suggests that he sing the "Doxology." And just as they are all singing the last line of this hymn, "Praise Father, Son, and Holy Ghost," quite another image of the deity is evoked by Burnett's description of Mrs. Sowerby, who now appears just inside the garden door (23:279–81).

Especially if one remembers Mrs. Sowerby's twelve children as well as her food gifts for Colin and Mary and other kinds of intercession on their behalf, her description here reminds one of a pagan earth mother or fertility goddess—suggested by her being framed by nature—and possibly the Virgin Mary as well—suggested by the color of her cloak: "With the ivy behind her, the sunlight drifting through the trees and dappling her blue cloak, and her nice fresh face smiling across the greenery, she was rather like a softly coloured illustration in one of Colin's books." Her gaze suggests a loving omniscience: "She had wonderful affectionate eyes which seemed to take everything in—

all of them, even Ben Weatherstaff and the 'creatures' and every flower that was in bloom." Being unexpected and remaining unnoticed until she is already inside the garden, her arrival has the suddenness of an apparition (23:281). After putting her blessing on all the new natural and human health to be found in the garden, Mrs. Sowerby confirms the universalist character of the garden ceremonies as well: "Th' Magic listened when tha' sung th' Doxology. It would ha' listened to anything tha'd sung. It was th' joy that mattered. Eh! lad, lad—what's names to th' Joy Maker" (23:285).

EXEMPLUM AND NARRATIVE STANCE

The influence of the exemplum on *The Secret Garden* can be seen in the last seven chapters not only in the children's garden religion but also in Burnett's increased preoccupation with the interpretation of her tale: being a didactic form like the fable or parable, the exemplum is often valued as much for its message as for its story. Sometimes this interpretation comes from an omniscient narrator, as when at the beginning of chapter 21 Colin's feeling that he will "live forever and ever" is explained. Similarly, the book's final chapter, chapter 27, begins with a paragraph on the power of the mind to affect one's physical and psychological health, reflecting Burnett's contacts with Christian Science. This paragraph is followed by three more that use Mary, Colin, and Mr. Craven as examples. In chapter 23 Colin himself becomes an interpreter during his oration about magic.

In addition to inserting an interpretive, omniscient narrator, Burnett uses other distancing techniques during the last seven chapters, as if to ask the reader to stand back from the story and contemplate its meaning as a whole. For most of the earlier chapters, Burnett's narrator had kept us fairly close to the action by looking over Mary's shoulder, telling us what she felt and thought, inviting us to experience the story with her. Now, we are given several other points of view in addition to that of an omniscient narrator. Much of the children's delight in making the manor adults believe that Colin is still sick is described by Dickon in an extended conversation with his mother, in chapter 24.

Later in that chapter Dickon narrates, complete with dialogue, his visit with a local athlete who had suggested exercises to strengthen Colin. And chapter 25 opens with six paragraphs from the robin's point of view: we are told how he and his mate feared for their eggs because Colin's awkward first steps reminded them of a cat "preparing to pounce." Colin learning to walk, the robin eventually realizes, is like a bird learning to fly, continuing the book's pattern of imagery that suggests that the garden is the children's nest (25:268–69).

Much of the book's last chapter is told from the point of view of Mr. Craven during his travels and eventual return to the Misselthwaite garden. Colin's healthy walk with his father from the garden to the manor in the final paragraphs of the book is narrated over the shoulder of Ben Weatherstaff looking out the kitchen window. Finally, in these last seven chapters there are patches of narrative carried primarily by dialogue and succinct description of action. In these scenes the narrator almost disappears behind the action, as in a play. We are occasionally and briefly told what Mary thought; what Colin thought we learn primarily from his own speeches.

The overt didacticism of the exemplum has gone out of fashion, and so the interpretive comments of Burnett's narrator during the last portion of her book are objectionable to some readers. In addition, the multiple points of view in these chapters and the resulting fact that we never get as close to Colin during his transformation as we did to Mary during hers can be seen as a break from the book's earlier coherence as well as an indication that Burnett was not so imaginatively engaged in Colin's character as she had been earlier in Mary's. These or similar observations are made especially by readers who are critical of the ideology regarding gender and class implicit in *The Secret Garden*.

9

Class and Gender

As described in chapter 3, within the past decade or so there has been considerable critical discussion of the portrayal of gender and class in *The Secret Garden*. The purpose of this chapter is not to retrace that critical discussion or to repeat relevant interpretations found in chapters 4 through 8. Instead, this chapter highlights aspects of the text that class and gender criticism has often overlooked and places interpretations articulated in earlier chapters within this critical context.

A class analysis of *The Secret Garden* should include an acknowledgment that with the exception of Mary, Colin, Mr. Craven, Mrs. Craven, and Dr. Craven, all of the characters individualized or developed in the novel belong to the working class—Martha, Dickon, and Susan Sowerby; Mrs. Medlock and Colin's nurse; the head gardener Mr. Roach and Ben Weatherstaff. Moreover, it is with these members of the working class that Mary and Colin are most often shown interacting, and, with the exception of Martha, they remain significant through the entire book. For example, a significant part of chapter 24 is devoted to a conversation in which Dickon tells his mother about the children's attempts to make the manor adults think Colin is still sick, and Mrs. Sowerby says she will send milk and bread to help them with their "play actin'" (24:255).

THE SOWERBYS' HARDSHIPS

The folk wisdom of the Sowerbys and their special concern for the manor children can evoke the complacent stereotype of the rural working class as happy naturals chiefly concerned with the welfare of their betters. This stereotype is encouraged by some of Martha Sowerby's descriptions. For example, she says that her siblings "tumble about on th' moor an' play there all day, an' mother says th' air of the moor fattens 'em. She says she believes they eat the grass same as th' wild ponies do" (4:30). Such statements are more than balanced, however, by Martha's frequent references to the Sowerbys' hardships, especially when compared with conditions in the manor. The Sowerby children stay much out of doors undoubtedly because the family of 14 is crowded into a cottage with only "four little rooms," a stark contrast to the manor with its near "a hundred rooms," most of which are "shut up and locked" (4:52–53). When rain keeps the Sowerby children inside, Martha says, even her "good-tempered" mother "gets fair moithered" (2:14).

Unlike the secret garden at Misselthwaite, Dickon's cottage garden is devoted primarily to the vegetables that his family needs, and Martha rarely misses an opportunity to point out the Sowerbys' limited diet. When Mary does not want to eat her breakfast, for example, Martha says that her own her siblings "scarce ever had their stomachs full in their lives" (4:31). Martha also gives Mary a lesson in comparative economics. When the child cannot think of how to spend her weekly allowance of a shilling, Martha points out that this is only a little less than the Sowerbys' weekly cottage rent, adding that "it's like pulling eye-teeth to get it" (9:85). Similarly dramatic comparisons are available to a mathematically inclined reader. Stopping at the Sowerby cottage on his way back to Misselthwaite, Mr. Craven, on impulse, gives the Sowerby children a golden sovereign, this pocket change being three times their father's weekly wages of 16 shillings (27:298, 4:30).

Although the lonely Mary and Colin are understandably infatuated by the idea of a family with 12 children, the economic discrepancy between cottage and manor is not entirely lost on them. Mary seems to recognize that the Sowerbys' buying Mary a skipping rope represents a sacrifice, noting that the "tuppence" came from Martha's wages and uttering an unprecedented "Thank you" (8:73). When Mrs. Sowerby sends food, Mary and Colin realize "that as Mrs. Sowerby had 14 people to provide food for she might not have enough to satisfy two extra appetites every day. So they asked her to let them send some of their shillings to buy things" (24:261). The novel also points out that being a Sowerby means having a limited formal education. Martha and Dickon can print but not write or read script, and Martha's comments about "blacks" indicate that she has derived her vision of the larger world primarily from religious tracts (9:85–86, 4:27).

THE LIFE OF A SERVANT

The Secret Garden avoids glamorizing working-class life also by indicating the personal sacrifices of being a wage earner. Martha gets only one day off each month, when she typically walks the five miles to and from the Sowerby cottage to help her mother (8:69–70). Mrs. Medlock appreciates her "comfortable well paid place as housekeeper," but she knows that "the only way in which she could keep it was to do at once what Mr. Archibald Craven told her to do. She never dared even to ask a question." Thus, she has to miss her niece's wedding because her master told her to go to London to get Mary (2:13).

With such a master, it is not surprising that his servants sometimes take advantage of his absence, living "a luxurious life below stairs, where there was a huge kitchen hung about with shining brass and pewter, and a large servants' hall where there were four or five abundant meals eaten every day, and where a great deal of lively romping went on when Mrs. Medlock was out of the way." This latter event is apparently frequent, for, after her uncle leaves, Mary notices that Mrs. Medlock seems "always to be in her comfortable housekeeper's sitting room down-stairs" (6:54). Thus, although protective of their positions, as when they cater to Colin to avoid being blamed for his relapse, the manor servants are not unduly self-sacrificing or subservient. This relaxation of the manor's class system, moreover, has the important result that Mary is exposed to the first person to set her in the right direction, Martha Sowerby. "If there was a grand missus at Misselthwaite" or a master paying attention to its affairs, Martha says, her dialect and "common" ways would have prevented her from working anywhere but the kitchen. "Mrs. Medlock gave me th' place out o' kindness," she tells Mary (4:26).

MRS. MEDLOCK

Mrs. Medlock herself provides an interesting case for class analysis. It is likely that her finding a place for Martha was a genuine act "o' kindness," for we learn that Mrs. Medlock and Susan Sowerby went to school together and have a continuing friendship—Dickon says that Mrs. Medlock always stops to visit his mother when she goes to Thwaite (19:198, 15:164). That she has the same "common" origin as the Sowerbys is punctuated by her occasional use of Yorkshire dialect, as when she is thinking, is caught off guard, or thinks no one can hear her. During her first encounter with Mary, for example, Mrs. Medlock thinks to herself, "a more marred-looking young one I never saw in my life," and Burnett emphasizes the dialectal nature of Mrs. Medlock's "thought" by adding, parenthetically, that "marred is a Yorkshire word and means spoiled and pettish" (2:14). Later, standing outside Colin's room and overhearing Mary's attempts to imitate Dickon's speech, Mrs. Medlock expresses her surprise in "rather broad Yorkshire herself because there was no one to hear her" (18:190).

Mrs. Medlock also sometimes uses dialect as a mark of class solidarity. During a good-natured interchange with the stationmaster near the beginning of the novel, she answers his "broad" pronunciation "with a Yorkshire accent herself" (3:19). Moreover, a comment she later makes to Dr. Craven can be interpreted as expressing a certain pride in her class origin. Mrs. Medlock quotes in dialect one of Mrs. Sowerby's wise sayings about child rearing. When Dr. Craven observes that Mrs. Sowerby is "a shrewd woman," Mrs. Medlock, "much pleased," acknowledges that "she's got a way of saying things." Then she adds, "Sometimes I've said to her, 'Eh! Susan, if you was a different woman an' didn't talk such broad Yorkshire I've seen the times when I should have said you was clever'" (19:199).

This last statement admits several interpretations. Taken at face value, it suggests that Mrs. Medlock has internalized the prejudice that class dialect and intelligence are related, that she is being condescending to Mrs. Sowerby and reminding the doctor of her own superiority. Taken ironically, however, Mrs. Medlock is paying Mrs. Sowerby a genuine complement as well as using her as an example to expose the folly of that class prejudice. This latter interpretation is supported by the fact that Mrs. Medlock has just let the doctor know that she shares Mrs. Sowerby's social origin—she had prefaced her quotation of Mrs. Sowerby by volunteering that she had gone to school with her. In addition, her statement about Mrs. Sowerby's broad Yorkshire and cleverness is itself in that dialect, and she gives every evidence of being proud as well as "fond" of Mrs. Sowerby (19:198).

THE GARDEN AS CLASSLESS EDEN

That Mrs. Sowerby as well as Martha and Dickon are "clever" the reader, along with Mary and Colin, has no doubt. And while Martha suffers because of the albeit relaxed social hierarchy within the manor—the footman and upper-housemaids make fun of her dialect (5:48)—class is worn lightly by Dickon and Susan Sowerby. Dickon would "be at home in Buckingham Palace or at the bottom of a coal mine," according to the head gardener, Mr. Roach (20:209). And when Mrs. Sowerby meets Colin for the first time in the garden, Burnett's narrator pointedly observes that she does "not say, 'Mester Colin,' but just 'dear lad'" (26:282). Moreover, Mary and Colin honor the Sowerbys by using their Yorkshire dialect when they work in the garden. Details such as this as well as the children's great admiration for Dickon and Susan Sowerby are probably what led Fred Inglis to see the secret garden community as a classless Eden.[1]

The secret garden does not erase the class distinctions of those who enter it, however, as can be seen in Mary's and Colin's contrasting initial responses to it. Although reared with ruling-class expectations in colonial India, Mary is now apparently entirely dependent on the charity of her wealthy relatives. Accordingly, when she shares her secret find with Dickon, she says, "I've stolen a garden. . . . It isn't mine," and despite asserting that she has a right to enjoy it because she is "the only one in the world who wants it to be alive," she feels a need to get Mr. Craven's permission to tend it (10:102–103, 12:121). When he first enters the garden, however, Colin establishes his role as the Misselthwaite heir by declaring "This is my garden" and planting a bush like a king. Colin gives orders to Dickon, Mary, and Ben Weatherstaff and later becomes the organizer of garden activities.

In so doing, according to critics such as Claudia Marquis, Heather Murray, and Jerry Phillips, Colin simply exchanges the tyranny of an invalid for the imperious ego of an estate master—all with the apparent approval of the author.[2] Clearly, this is a supportable reading, especially given the adulation of aristocracy and royalty found in some of Burnett's subsequent works, such as *The Lost Prince* (1915), *The Head of the House of Coombe* (1922), and *Robin* (1922). Nevertheless, the implicit attitude toward Colin's egocentric behavior in the last part of *The Secret Garden* is more complex than it might at first appear.

PLAYING RAJAH

Early in their relationship, after observing Colin's insistence that he can make the servants do what he wants, Mary says that he reminds her of an Indian rajah. And Colin continues to give orders like a rajah, a word used more than 10 times in chapters 19 and 20 depicting Dickon's visit to his room and the children's plans for Colin's first trip to the garden. "In his most Rajah-like manner," for example, Colin gives orders to his nurse about Dickon's impending visit: "You are not to begin playing with the animals in the servants' hall and keep them there. I want them here" (19:202). "Rather like a Rajah," Colin tells his doctor that he will go outside without his nurse (19:195–96). And because the children want to keep their garden visits a secret, Colin orders the head gardener to keep everyone out of the way when Mary and Dickon wheel him outside. During the gardener's command appearance, "the young Rajah" looks "his servitor over," gives his orders, and then waves his hand while pronouncing, "You have my permission to go, Roach" (20:210-11).

The indulgent view of Colin's rajah-like behavior adopted by Burnett's narrator can be interpreted as a sign of the book's tilt toward an upper-class perspective. It is also a child's play-acting, however, that elicits the narrator's smile, a game participated in by Mary, who coaches Colin on what "you say in India when you have finished talking and want people to go" (20:211). In addition, some light humor is apparently intended in this reversal of usual child and adult roles. Just as Mary earlier succeeded with Colin where adults had failed, Colin now orders the adults to let him go outside as they earlier could not convince him to do, a point noted later by the doctor (24:259). Various kinds of role reversal, such as children keeping secrets from adults who typically keep secrets from them, as well as children caring for each other better than they have been cared for by adults, have been cited by critics such as Alison Lurie and Rosemary Threadgold as contributing in a major way to the book's continuing appeal.[3]

Moreover, while Burnett's narrator finds mild humor in Colin's lordly behavior, a more critical point of view comes from the servants, whose role in Colin's play-acting, of course, is more than just a game. From the beginning, we have been informed that they take a dim view of him. Mary's early voiced opinion that Colin is "a very spoiled boy," for example, had elicited Martha's frank observation that he's "th' worst young nowt [good-for-nothing] as ever was!" (14:143). Later, within the servants' hall, there had been "a great deal of joking about the unpopular young recluse who, as the cook said, 'had found his master [in Mary], and good for him.'" "And the butler, who was a man with a family, had more than once expressed his opinion that the invalid would be all the better 'for a good hiding'" (19:202).

Even after "savage little Mary" has quelled Colin's tantrums (17:179), however, his upstairs behavior does not escape downstairs criticism if the opinions of the head gardener, Mr. Roach, and the head housekeeper, Mrs. Medlock, are any indication. Mr. Roach treats with some sarcasm the royal airs of his young master, saying to himself as he answers Colin's summons, "Well, well . . . what's to do now? His

Royal Highness that wasn't to be looked at calling up a man he's never set eyes on." As he leaves Colin's room, Mr. Roach observes to Mrs. Medlock that the boy has "got a fine lordly way with him, hasn't he? You'd think he was a whole Royal Family rolled into one—Prince Consort and all." The disdain in Mrs. Medlock's response is more direct. "Eh! . . . we've had to let him trample all over every one of us since he had feet and he thinks that's what folks was born for." Because she says "he thinks" rather than "he thought" and because she had earlier acknowledged to Mr. Roach that Colin has already changed for the better, her caustic criticism can be interpreted as referring to Colin's current rajah-like behavior, as just displayed to Mr. Roach (20:208–209, 211).

BEN WEATHERSTAFF

Being so ready to repeat "Yes, sir!" and to obey the boy's orders, Ben Weatherstaff would seem to be an exception to the irreverent attitude most of Misselthwaite's servants adopt toward Colin. This difference results in large part because Ben has a more personal interest in the boy, who resembles his mother, someone the gardener had much loved. Wanting to be sure that the recovering invalid does not hurt himself, Ben shows his "shrewd understanding" by finding a way to remain in the garden (22:232). Perceiving the children's dismay that an adult has discovered their secret, he assures a continuing welcome by joining their games. As Sara Crewe had imagined herself a princess, Colin finds that being wheeled around the garden is like "being taken in state round the country of a magic king and queen [which could be interpreted as Dickon and Mary] and shown all the mysterious riches it contained" (21:219). Later Ben Weatherstaff, who had been watching over the wall, suggests that Colin plant a rose bush "same as th' king does when he goes to a new place" (22:235). In the following scenes Ben pretends to be a saluting sailor and a parishioner in Colin's "church" (23:242–44, 247–48).

In these scenes Weatherstaff may seem a rustic buffoon, offering Jem Fettleworth and her "drunken brute" of a husband as a case for

Colin's "sinetifik 'speriment" in the magic power of language and falling asleep during Colin's chanting after what Ben calls the boy's "sermon" (23:244–45, 248). Ben's comments and behavior, however, can also be interpreted as a commentary on Colin's pomposity, perhaps deliberate on Ben's part. For example, when Colin says how much he likes to lecture, Ben responds, "Th' best thing about lecturin' . . . is that a chap can get up an' say aught he pleases an' no other chap can answer him back. I wouldn't be agin' lecturin' a bit mysel' sometimes" (26:276).

COLIN UNMASKED

This comment comes at the beginning of the book's penultimate chapter, in which Colin finally realizes he is well and Mrs. Sowerby enters the garden. In this chapter the closest Colin gets to his earlier rajah game is to hold out his hand to Mrs. Sowerby with a "flushed royal shyness" (26:282). Moreover, while he acknowledges his own role in his recovery by saying that the "Magic works best when you work yourself," he mainly wants to be thankful to that power, which he acknowledges to be greater than himself (26:277). In this chapter Colin is well enough to give up his mask of self-importance and allow others to see him as he really is, a still insecure and needy child. He asks Mrs. Sowerby's assurance that his resemblance to his mother will make his father like him, and he expresses the wish that she could be his mother "as well as Dickon's" (26:282, 286). In short, it is possible to interpret this penultimate chapter as a suggestion that, like Mary before him, Colin is becoming less egocentric and learning to have his vision less distorted by class.

MARY'S CHANGE

The apparently unqualified assent given Colin's egocentrism in the last part of the book is often noted also by gender critics of *The Secret Garden,* such as Elizabeth Lennox Keyser and Lissa Paul as well as

Marquis and Murray.[4] Such critics typically lament also that during the last third of the book a less assertive Mary gradually recedes into the background. It is certainly true that her last action is losing a race to Colin as the children exit the garden and that she is almost forgotten in the subsequent pages portraying the reunion between "Master Colin" and "the Master of Misselthwaite" (27:302–306). Mary does not, however, lose all of her spirit in the last third of the book. For example, she "obstinately" protests Ben Weatherstaff's "outraged" "harangue" in which he blames her for bringing Colin into the garden and thus endangering his health (21:224–25). Although she has become Colin's staunch advocate and admirer, she is still willing to chide him; she shares with him her opinion that he is "a rude little brute," telling him that she would never have been polite to him for 10 years as his doctor has been (23:237–38). She also continues to be an initiator of action, suggesting and leading Colin's first exploration of the many-roomed manor.

Moreover, Mary's own change is not ignored in the chapters focusing primarily on Colin's. After he notices the portrait of "the plain little girl" in the family gallery, Colin tells Mary, "She looks rather like you, Mary—not as you look now but as you looked when you came here. Now you are a great deal fatter and better looking" (25:272–73). Archibald Craven's absorption with his son apparently allows him to take no notice of Mary, but in the previous chapter Susan Sowerby had not been so negligent. After Ben Weatherstaff asks her to give close examination to Colin's strong legs, Mrs. Sowerby volunteers a compliment about Mary's healthy beauty just as had Mrs. Medlock somewhat earlier after Dr. Craven had declared Colin "a new creature" (26:283, 24:265).

The fact that Mrs. Sowerby and Mrs. Medlock focus primarily on Mary's beauty might bother some readers who object that *The Secret Garden* ultimately reinforces conventional gender roles, an objection supported by a comparison of Colin's and Mary's activities in the secret garden. Colin is soon setting up experiments and organizing activities he expects the others to join; he makes the garden his training ground for future careers as athlete, scientist, and lecturer. Mary is more nurturant and cooperative. Weeding, planting, and watching the garden grow are sufficiently rewarding activities; she invites Dickon to join her the first time she meets him and later plans and enjoys bringing Colin in. We hear nothing of Mary's future plans, the garden apparently serving as a laboratory for homemaking and parenting skills.

FEMALE NURTURANCE

The Secret Garden does not argue that the ability to be nurturant is an inborn female trait. Mary learns from Dickon how to care for sprouting plants and baby animals; Ben Weatherstaff often behaves like a good parent while Mrs. Medlock has little interest in children; and Archibald Craven's willingness to become nurturant is suggested to be the source of his own salvation. Nevertheless, the cooperative chain of nurturance that brings about the healing of Colin and his father—Martha, Ben, the robin, Mary, Mrs. Sowerby, and Colin's dead mother—is primarily female. At the heart of the book lies the secret garden itself as a symbol of female generativity.

Readers' responses to Burnett's portrayal of gender are thus likely to depend in large part on their attitude toward the claim that cooperation and nurturance are salutary features of female identity, a claim about which feminists are often divided. According to Marquis, for example, *The Secret Garden* "clearly promotes a conception of motherhood as power of a sort: the power of fecundity, of giving; ostensibly it honors the mother, but never observes that this is actually a cultural procedure by which women are subordinated and consumed"; "Burnett was no more able to construct a literary system that does other than grant privileged status to the male then Freud was in his theorising of psychoanalysis."[5] Other critics have found in its portrayal of female generativity and nurturance a source of the book's continuing appeal. For Elizabeth Francis, Burnett's portrayal of the secret garden as "maternal space" breaks through the "surface of her plot [where] male authority appears to replace female."[6] Adrian Gunther develops this argument and asserts that the book recasts the Edenic myth—"it is Adam/Archibald who commits the sin that causes the expulsion from the garden," while "Lilias or Eve is the real power behind the garden."[7] After a discussion of how the garden and manor come to represent the still-nurturant Lilias herself, I have elsewhere argued that "at some level, the reader, along with Mary, Colin, and finally even Archibald Craven, reenacts the usually repressed desire to explore the secret mysteries of the mother's body as well as her soul."[8]

Jerry Phillips has called *The Secret Garden* "a richly confused text" characterized by "ideological dissonance."[9] Critics who excavate and describe this dissonance often explain the book's continuing status as a classic by observing that what they recall from their childhood reading is primarily the first part of the book, Mary's discovery of the garden and exploration of the manor. Often added is a version of the following conjecture, here articulated by U. C. Knoepflmacher: "By successfully screening out discordancies that an adult reader cannot as easily dismiss, the child reader can always be more selective."[10] Clearly there is much to be said for this conjecture, but anyone who reads widely in the criticism of a text as complex as *The Secret Garden* is likely to discover that, having their own ideologies and personal interests, adult readers can be selective, too.

Approaches to Teaching

The characters and events in *The Secret Garden* probably have the greatest appeal for children between the ages of 9 and 11, or fourth through sixth grades. Because of the book's length, complexity, and dialect, however, not all children in these grades might be able to read it unassisted. Thus it is an excellent book to be read aloud by the teacher, the children following in their own copies if available. This project will take three to four weeks if one reads aloud 30 to 40 minutes daily, five days a week. If children are asked to read the book on their own, their appreciation will be greatly enhanced if individual assignments of several chapters each are followed by class discussion to answer questions and articulate expectations for the next chapters.

WRITING PROJECTS

Various writing or drawing projects could stimulate interest before reading the book. Children might be asked to imagine a secret place where they could be alone with friends and do what they like; if they choose a garden, they could describe flowers or anything else they would like in it as well as what features would make the garden "secret." Alternatively, children could be asked to imagine a large house that would be fun to explore, including parts that would be secret to someone casually walking through it, parts that might seem frightening, parts they would especially like. They could even write a story about someone who comes to this house as a guest, perhaps including a ghost or two.

Children of this age can be encouraged to think about the characters, plot, setting, and themes of a book by comparing it with other works having some similar features. Traditional tales, other short stories, picture books, and poems might be studied at appropriate points before, while, or after the book is read aloud. For example, children might be told of Burnett's love of folk tales, especially the Cinderella tale. The teacher might read or tell several variants, including the Grimms' version and the Russian "Vasilisa." In these latter tales the magic that helps the protagonist is connected to her dead mother, a motif found in the role of Colin's dead mother in *The Secret Garden*, as I discuss in chapter 8. The children might notice other features of Burnett's story frequently found in fairy tales, such as magic, marvelous transformations, and a happy ending involving a family reunion, as in "Hansel and Gretel." This would be an excellent opportunity to read some folk tales from India, such as "How Sun, Moon, and Wind Went Out to Dinner" (in Joanna Cole, *Best-Loved Folktales of the World* [Doubleday, 1982]), and Burnett's use of the seasonal cycle to underscore the transformation of her characters could be compared with that in Hans Christian Andersen's "The Ugly Duckling."

COMPLEMENTARY CHILDREN'S WORKS

A similar use of the seasonal cycle is often found also in picture and illustrated books, such as Virginia Lee Burton's *The Little House* (1942) and William Steig's *Sylvester and the Magic Pebble* (1969), which concludes with a family reunion. The Greek myth of Demeter and Persephone explains the origin of the seasonal cycle and dramatizes a mother's love for her child. One might choose Penelope Proddow's *Demeter and Persephone*, illustrated by Barbara Cooney (1972) or Charlene Sprenak's adaptation in *Lost Goddesses of Early Greece* (1981), in which Persephone voluntarily spends winter in the underworld because of her compassion for the dead. In *Daughter of*

Earth (1984), Gerald McDermott has illustrated the Roman version of this myth. In addition to making comparisons with Colin's magical mother, children could discuss how Susan Sowerby resembles Demeter or Ceres, especially in chapter 26, "It's Mother!" For a complementary portrait of a woman's life, the never-married protagonist in Barbara Cooney's *Miss Rumphius* (1982) enjoys world travel before leaving a legacy of flowers. For a different kind of special place, Faith Ringgold's *Tar Beach* pictures how a girl's imagination is excited by starry nights viewed from the roof of a New York skyscraper (1991).

Any good anthology of poems for children will offer a number that highlight some aspect of *The Secret Garden.* Chapters about the robin, Dickon's animals, and other garden creatures could be combined with choral reading of the poems about birds and insects in Paul Fleischman's *I Am Phoenix* and *Joyful Noise,* both subtitled *Poems for Two Voices* (1985, 1988). In the latter book the portrayal of maternal care in "The Digger Wasp" is especially pertinent.

Longer books can be combined with *The Secret Garden* in a semester-long reading program. One might well precede it with Burnett's somewhat more accessible *A Little Princess* (1905), in which the use of the Cinderella tale is more obvious, and the use and meaning of "Magic" in the two books can be compared. As a bridge to the role of nature in *The Secret Garden,* one might use Burnett's short parable *The Land of the Blue Flower,* newly illustrated by Judith Ann Griffith in 1993. Children will enjoy Burnett's descriptions of her own favorite childhood gardens in chapters 3 and 14 of her 1893 memoir, *The One I Knew the Best of All,* sometimes available in public libraries. Finally, the teacher might read passages from one of the two biographies written for children, *Happily Ever After,* by Constance Buel Burnett, and *Frances Hodgson Burnett,* by Angelica S. Carpenter and Jean Shirley. The latter is generously illustrated with photographs and plates from original editions of some of Burnett's books.

More contemporary books might also be paired with *The Secret Garden.* In Katherine Paterson's *Bridge to Terabithia* (1977), for example, a boy and girl find friendship in their secret place in the woods;

the book also ends with a death and a renewal. The barn in E. B. White's *Charlotte's Web* (1952) can be seen as a special place much like the secret garden. This book, too, uses the seasons to understand the cycle of life and death. Older children will find that the mysterious, past-haunted houses found in *The Secret Garden* and Virginia Hamilton's *The House of Dies Drear* (1968) have some provocative similarities and differences. Similarly for older children, Jean Little's autobiography, *Little by Little* (1987), describes how *The Secret Garden* helped her deal with her sight impairment during childhood and later influenced her as a children's writer.

CLASS DISCUSSION

The reading of *The Secret Garden* itself will elicit many questions from children, usually the best place to begin a discussion. If the book is being read aloud to children without their own copies, careful listening can be encouraged by giving each a slip of paper with a key sentence or two from the book, one such passage from each chapter. At the end of each session, the students whose sentences have occurred read them aloud, providing a basis for discussion. For example, in chapter 1, one might choose "she saw a little snake gliding along and watching her with eyes like jewels. She was not frightened, because he was a harmless little thing" (1:6). This passage could stimulate discussion of the book's setting: living in India, Mary was probably accustomed to snakes and could identify them. One might ask for other reasons Burnett included this detail: the fact that even the snake was leaving her emphasizes Mary's isolation.

Larger questions can be used to stimulate interest and discussion. Children could be asked to look in early parts of the book for all the persons and other parts of Mary's new environment that somehow provide a mirror for her, such as the robin, Ben Weatherstaff, the portrait of the plain little girl, the garden, Archibald Craven, and Colin. Throughout the book children could be asked to look for mysteries or secrets in addition to the more obvious ones, such as Mary's mother keeping her daughter a secret from many, the family of mice

Mary finds in a cushion in a remote room in the manor, and Colin's not telling anyone of his fear that he will die. In the latter part of the book children could discuss the role in Colin's recovery played by Mary, Dickon, Ben Weatherstaff, Susan Sowerby, and Colin's dead mother. This would be a good time to introduce the Cinderella variants and Demeter myths. Earlier discussions of what the garden means to Mary, Colin, and his parents can lead to an appreciation for the various symbolic meanings the garden has accrued by the end of the novel.

ADAPTATIONS IN OTHER MEDIA

After reading the book, the class could view one or more of the movie versions, the 1987 and 1993 adaptations being readily available on videocassette. Changes from the book—such as having an unrelated Mary and Colin eventually marry in the 1987 television film or omitting Susan Sowerby in the 1993 movie—can lead to awareness of how character and plot changes affect a story's meaning and impact as well as why the different media encourage book authors and film directors to make different choices. If the magic role of Colin's mother has been discussed, students will enjoy hearing the cast album of the 1991 Broadway musical, in which she plays a major role as an on-stage ghost; available on compact disk or cassette (Columbia, CK 48817, 1991), the album uses dialogue to connect the songs and provides a written copy of the lyrics so that someone familiar with the book can easily follow without having seen the musical. The entire script by Marsha Norman and Lucy Simon is also available (Theatre Communications Group, 1992).

PROVIDING HISTORICAL CONTEXT

Children will better understand many of the characters and their interactions assisted by a brief description of the British empire and the class system in both colonial India and England. When children ask why Mary and Colin did not go to school, they can be informed that in wealthy families young children were usually taught at home by a tutor or governess; older boys were usually sent to boarding schools, while girls typically finished their education at home, learning the skills and refinements expected of a wife in charge of servants as well as her own children. In contrast, working class children typically learned little more than basic literacy skills in schools especially designed for them; the necessity of working for their parents or, sometimes, in factories usually meant that their time in school was severely limited.

This background knowledge will help explain the attitudes toward race, class, and gender in *The Secret Garden*. Martha's comments about "blacks" (4:27–28, 8:72), for example, result in large part from what her limited reading has taught her as well as from her natural curiosity about people who are different from herself. Children also might be asked how Mary's and Colin's attitudes toward themselves and other characters have been affected by the assumption that they were born into a superior class and whether there is any change in their attitudes as the book progresses. Discussions of class and gender could also be initiated by asking children to conjecture about what happened to Colin, Mary, and Dickon when they grew up and how their lives might be different if they lived today.

Many American children will find Burnett's use of the Yorkshire dialect a "foreign" distraction. They might be reminded that America, too, has regional dialects that are less obvious in the more homogenized language typically used, for example, by national television personalities. Similarly, the upper class of Britain was educated to speak a version of English less marked by regional dialect than that spoken by persons who spent their entire lives in one region. Dialect was thus a signal of class as well as regional origin, though, for a variety of reasons a person might be bilingual. Manor servants normally would be expected to avoid regional dialect when working with the master and his family, although, like Mrs. Medlock, they would sometimes use it in other contexts. Somewhat similarly, Mary and, though less often, Colin, sometimes use Yorkshire dialect to express their admiration of and friendship with Dickon, and Dickon avoids dialect when he quotes Mary to his mother (24:255).

TEACHING *THE SECRET GARDEN* TO ADULTS

The Secret Garden is often studied in college or university children's literature classrooms, where it is usually enjoyed by most students. In my classes I use many of the methods just described, partly because I model for future teachers approaches they will be able to use and partly because they often ask many of the same questions asked by the classes of fourth graders who have discussed *The Secret Garden* with me. Conversely, I have found that the fourth graders could discuss virtually all aspects of the book examined in my university classrooms, though not with as much textual elaboration.

The Secret Garden works well with either of the most widely used principles of course organization, historical or by genre. Historical studies could emphasize the book's use of the earlier exemplum form and Romantic view of nature coupled with its forward-looking child psychology. A genre approach might note that it has the combination of realism and fairy-tale fantasy found in much fiction for children. Finally, because of its own provocative complexity as well as an increasing scholarly appreciation for children's literature itself, *The Secret Garden* has occasionally been taught in courses focusing primarily on adult literature. As suggested in earlier discussions of recent criticism of *The Secret Garden,* the book would fit well in a women's literature course, especially compared with the frequently taught *Jane Eyre,* by Charlotte Brontë. *The Secret Garden* could be used as well in a course on late-nineteenth-century Romanticism or turn-of-the-century literature about the British empire.

When *The Secret Garden* appeared in 1911, as pointed out in chapter 3, a number of reviewers noted its potential appeal for adults as well as children. History has confirmed the validity of this prediction. *The Secret Garden* merits study in classrooms of adults as well as of children.

Notes and References

2. The Secret Garden as a Classic

1. Ann Thwaite, *Waiting for the Party: The Life of Frances Hodgson Burnett 1849–1924* (New York: Charles Scribner's Sons, 1974), 220; *New York Times,* 30 October 1924, 19, 1; 31 October 1924, 18, 5.

2. Louise Seaman Bechtel, "The Giant in Children," *Atlantic Monthly,* 1927; reprinted in *Books in Search of Children: Speeches and Essays by Louise Seaman Bechtel,* ed. Virginia Haviland (New York: Macmillan, 1969), 145–46.

3. John Rowe Townsend, *Written for Children: An Outline of English Children's Literature* (New York: Lothrop, Lee and Shepard, 1965), 75.

4. Jerry Griswold, "Positive Thinking: *The Secret Garden,*" in *Audacious Kids: Coming of Age in America's Classic Children's Books* (New York: Oxford University Press, 1992), 264–65.

5. Alison Lurie, "Happy Endings: Frances Hodgson Burnett," in *Don't Tell the Grown-ups: Why Kids Love the Books They Do* (New York: Avon, 1990), 143.

6. "Greta Garbo: The Legendary Star's Secret Garden in New York," *Architectural Digest* 49, no. 4 (April 1992): 120–29; Anna Wintour, "Her Secret Garden," review of glass-bead jewelry by Jessica Rose, *New York,* 31 January 1983, 42–43; Paul Brach, "[Arshile] Gorky's Secret Garden," *Art in America* 69 (October 1981): 122–24; Cynthia Brouse, "Secret Garden: Sweet Scents of Success in Giftware," *Canadian Business* 59 (December 1986): 155; Deborah Erickson, "Secret Garden: Cell Culture May Provide a Unique Route to Taxology," *Scientific American* 265, no. 4 (October 1991): 121–22; Suzanne M. Wilson, "The Secret Garden of Teacher Education," *Phi-Delta-Kappan* 72, no. 3 (November 1990): 204–209; Anne Lundin, "Secret Gardens: The Literature of Childhood," *Childhood Education* 67, no. 4 (Summer 1991): 215–17.

7.   Anita T. Sullivan, *"The Secret Garden," Kenyon Review* 11 (Spring 1989): 101–102.

8.   Doris B. Wallace, "Secret Gardens and Other Symbols of Gender in Literature," *Metaphor and Symbolic Activity* 3 (1988): 143.

9.   Ruth Barton, "T. S. Eliot's Secret Garden," *Notes and Queries* 31 (1984): 512–14; Christopher Heywood, "Frances Hodgson Burnett's *The Secret Garden:* A Possible Source for T. S. Eliot's 'Rose Garden,'" *Yearbook of English Studies* 7 (1977): 166–71; Alison White, "Tap-Roots into a Rose Garden," *Children's Literature* 1 (1972): 74–76; Judith Plotz, "Secret Garden II, or *Lady Chatterley's Lover* as Palimpsest," *Children's Literature Association Quarterly* 19 (Spring 1994): 15–19; Kathleen Verduin, *"Lady Chatterley* and *The Secret Garden:* Lawrence's Homage to Mrs. Hodgson Burnett," *D. H. Lawrence Review* 17 (Spring 1984): 61–66.

10.   Frank Luther Mott, *Golden Multitudes: The Story of Best Sellers in the United States* (New York: R. R. Bowker, 1947), 312–13, 324–25.

11.   For the parallels between *The Secret Garden* and *Bridge to Terabithia,* I am indebted to my colleague Joel Chaston, especially his paper "Pine Groves and Pumpkin Patches: Katherine Paterson's 'Secret Gardens,'" read at the annual meeting of the Children's Literature Association, 3 June 1994, in Springfield, Missouri.

12.   Katherine Paterson, *Gates of Excellence: On Reading and Writing Books for Children* (New York: E. P. Dutton, 1981), 104; Katherine Paterson, *The Spying Heart: More Thoughts on Reading and Writing Books for Children* (New York: E. P. Dutton, 1989), 109.

3. Critical Reception

1.   *Bookman* 41 Supplement (1911): 103; *American Library Association Booklist* 8 (October 1911): 76.

2.   *Bookman* 34 (October 1911): 183.

3.   *Bookman* 41 Supplement (1911): 103.

4.   Thwaite, *Waiting for the Party,* 222.

5.   *Athenaeum,* 18 November 1911, 621.

6.   Francis J. Molson, "Frances Hodgson Burnett (1848–1924)," *American Literary Realism* 8 (Winter 1975): 39–41.

7.   Marghanita Laski, *Mrs. Ewing, Mrs. Molesworth and Mrs. Hodgson Burnett* (New York: Oxford University Press, 1951), 87, 88, 91.

8.   Lillian H. Smith, *The Unreluctant Years: A Critical Approach to Children's Literature* (New York: American Library Association, 1953); Eleanor Cameron, *The Green and Burning Tree: On the Writing and Enjoyment of Children's Books* (Boston: Little, Brown, 1962).

9. Roger Lancelyn Green, *Tellers of Tales: An Account of Children's Favorite Authors from 1839 to the Present Day, Their Books and How They Came to Write Them, Together with an Appendix and Indexes Giving the Titles and Dates of These Books* (Leicester: Edmund Ward, 1953), 10–11.

10. Roger Lancelyn Green, "The Golden Age of Children's Books," in *Only Connect: Readings in Children's Literature,* ed. Sheila Egoff (Toronto: Oxford University Press, 1980), 10–11.

11. Roger Lancelyn Green, *Tellers of Tales: British Authors of Children's Books from 1800 to 1964* (New York: Franklin Watts, 1965).

12. Townsend, *Written for Children,* 71–72, 76, 69; John Rowe Townsend, *Written for Children: An Outline of English-Language Children's Literature,* 4th rev. ed. (New York: HarperCollins, 1990), 63–66.

13. Thwaite, *Waiting for the Party,* 220–21.

14. Robert Lee White, "Little Lord Fauntleroy as Hero," in *Challenges in American Culture,* ed. Ray B. Brown, Larry N. Landrum, and William Bottorff (Bowling Green: Bowling Green University Popular Press, 1970), 209–16.

15. White, "Tap-Roots into a Rose Garden."

16. Molson, "Frances Hodgson Burnett (1848–1924)."

17. Phyllis Bixler Koppes, "Tradition and the Individual Talent of Frances Hodgson Burnett: A Generic Analysis of *Little Lord Fauntleroy, A Little Princess,* and *The Secret Garden,*" *Children's Literature* 7 (1978): 191–207.

18. Stephen D. Roxburgh, " 'Our First World': Form and Meaning in *The Secret Garden,*" *Children's Literature in Education* 10 (Fall 1979): 120–30; Rosemary Threadgold, *"The Secret Garden:* An Appreciation of Frances Hodgson Burnett as a Novelist for Children," *Children's Literature in Education* 10 (Fall 1979): 113–19.

19. Madelon S. Gohlke, "Re-reading *The Secret Garden,*" *College English* 41 (April 1980): 894–902.

20. Fred Inglis, *The Promise of Happiness: Value and Meaning in Children's Fiction* (Cambridge: Cambridge University Press, 1981), 3, 112.

21. Elizabeth Francis, "Feminist Versions of Pastoral," *Children's Literature Association Quarterly* 7 (Winter 1982): 7–10.

22. Phyllis Bixler, *Frances Hodgson Burnett* (Boston: G. K. Hall, 1984), 99–101.

23. Roderick McGillis, " 'Secrets' and 'Sequence' in Children's Stories," *Studies in the Literary Imagination* 18 (Fall 1985): 35–46; Gillian Adams, "Secrets and Healing Magic in *The Secret Garden,*" in *Triumphs of the Spirit in Children's Literature,* ed. Francelia Butler and Richard Rotert (Hamden, Conn.: Library Professional Publications, Shoe String Press, 1986), 42–54.

Notes and References

24. M. Sarah Smedman, "Springs of Hope: Recovery of Primordial Time in 'Mythic' Novels for Young Readers," *Children's Literature* 16 (1988): 91–107.

25. Elizabeth Lennox Keyser, "'Quite Contrary': Frances Hodgson Burnett's *The Secret Garden,*" *Children's Literature* 11 (1983): 1–13; U. C. Knoepflmacher, "Little Girls without Their Curls: Female Aggression in Victorian Children's Literature," *Children's Literature* 11 (1983): 14–31.

26. Lissa Paul, "Enigma Variations: What Feminist Theory Knows about Children's Literature," *Signal* 54 (September 1987): 186–201.

27. Phyllis Bixler, "Gardens, Houses, and Nurturant Power in *The Secret Garden,*" in *Romanticism and Children's Literature in Nineteenth-Century England,* ed. James Holt McGavran, Jr. (Athens and London: University of Georgia Press, 1991), 208–24; Adrian Gunther, *"The Secret Garden* Revisited," *Children's Literature in Education* 25 (September 1994): 167–68.

28. Phyllis Bixler, *"The Secret Garden* 'Misread': The Broadway Musical as Creative Interpretation," *Children's Literature* 22 (1994): 101–23.

29. Lurie, "Happy Endings," 142.

30. Griswold, "Positive Thinking," 211.

31. Barbara R. Almond, M. D., *"The Secret Garden:* A Therapeutic Metaphor," *Psychoanalytic Study of the Child* 45 (1990): 480, 487, 490.

32. Claudia Marquis, "The Power of Speech: Life in *The Secret Garden,*" *AUMLA: Journal of the Australasian Universities Language and Literature Association* 68 (November 1987): 163–87.

33. Heather Murray, "Frances Hodgson Burnett's *The Secret Garden:* The Organ(ic)ized World," in *Touchstones: Reflections on the Best in Children's Literature,* ed. Perry Nodelman (West Lafayette, Ind.: Children's Literature Association, 1985), 37.

34. Jerry Phillips, "The Mem Sahib, the Worthy, the Rajah and His Minions: Some Reflections on the Class Politics of *The Secret Garden,*" *Lion and the Unicorn* 17 (December 1993): 185, 176, 193.

35. In her article praising mythic themes in *The Secret Garden,* M. Sarah Smedman calls "the fictional world of *The Secret Garden*" "unquestionably class-bound" (98). In my "Gardens, Houses, and Nurturant Power in *The Secret Garden,*" I make the same point, and, in describing houses as images of economic power, I discuss the more explicit critique of patriarchal restraints on women in some of Burnett's other fiction (214–16).

36. Marquis, "The Power of Speech," 169–77.

37. Murray, "The Organ(ic)ized World," 40.

38. Humphrey Carpenter, *Secret Gardens: A Study of the Golden Age of Children's Literature* (Boston: Houghton Mifflin, 1985), x, 188.

4. "Mistress Mary, Quite Contrary" (Chapters 1–8)

1. *The Secret Garden,* ed. Dennis Butts (Oxford and New York: Oxford University Press, 1987), 1; hereafter cited in the text.

2. Keyser, "'Quite Contrary,'" and Knoepflmacher, "Little Girls without Their Curls."

3. Thwaite, *Waiting for the Party,* 221; Almond, "A Therapeutic Metaphor," 478.

4. Almond, "A Therapeutic Metaphor," 489.

5. Almond, "A Therapeutic Metaphor," 489.

6. Griswold, "Positive Thinking," 202.

5. "Might I Have a Bit of Earth?" (Chapters 9–12)

1. Almond, "A Therapeutic Metaphor," 493.

2. Plotz, "Secret Garden II," 17–18.

6. "I Am Colin" (Chapters 13–20)

1. Griswold, "Positive Thinking," 207.

2. Adams, "Secrets and Healing Magic in *The Secret Garden.*"

7. Nest Building (Chapters 13–20)

1. Verduin, *"Lady Chatterley* and *The Secret Garden;"* Plotz, "Secret Garden II," 19.

9. Class and Gender

1. Inglis, *The Promise of Happiness,* 112.

2. Marquis, "The Power of Speech"; Murray, "The Organ(ic)ized World"; Phillips, "The Mem Sahib, the Worthy, the Rajah and His Minions."

3. Lurie, "Happy Endings; Threadgold, "An Appreciation of Frances Hodgson Burnett as a Novelist for Children."

4. Keyser, "'Quite Contrary'"; Paul, "Enigma Variations."

5. Marquis, "The Power of Speech," 184.

6. Francis, "Feminist Versions of Pastoral," 9.

7. Gunther, *"The Secret Garden* Revisited," 166–67.

8. Bixler, "Gardens, Houses, and Nurturant Power," 223.

9. Phillips, "The Mem Sahib, the Worthy, the Rajah and His Minions," 187.

10. Knoepflmacher, "Little Girls Without Their Curls," 31.

Selected Bibliography

Primary Works

Giovanni and the Other Children Who Have Made Stories. New York: Scribners, 1892. Published in England as *Children I Have Known*. London: J. R. Osgood, 1892; London: McIlvaine, 1892.

In the Closed Room. New York: Grosset & Dunlap, 1904; London: Hodder & Stoughton, 1904.

In the Garden. Boston: Medici Society, 1925.

The Land of the Blue Flower. New York: Moffat Yard, 1909; London: Putnam, 1912.

Little Lord Fauntleroy. New York: Scribners, 1886; London: Warne, 1886.

A Little Princess: Being the Whole Story of Sara Crewe Now Told for the First Time. New York: Scribners, 1905; London: Warne, 1905.

Little Saint Elizabeth and Other Stories. New York: Scribners, 1890; London: Warne, 1890.

The Lost Prince. New York: Century, 1915; London: Hodder & Stoughton, 1915.

My Robin. New York: Stokes, 1912; London: Putnam, 1913.

The One I Knew the Best of All: A Memory of the Mind of a Child. New York: Scribners, 1893; London: Warne, 1893.

Piccino and Other Child Stories. New York: Scribners, 1894. Published in England as *The Captain's Youngest*. London: Warne, 1894.

Sara Crewe and Editha's Burglar. London: Warne, 1888.

The Secret Garden. New York: Stokes, 1911; London: Heinemann, 1911.

Two Little Pilgrims' Progress: A Story of the City Beautiful. New York: Scribners, 1895; London: Warne, 1895.

Secondary Works

Books

Bixler, Phyllis. *Frances Hodgson Burnett.* Boston: G. K. Hall, 1984. Surveys Burnett's fiction, evaluating her contributions to the realist novel and popular adult fiction as well as children's literature; includes some feminist readings.

Bruno, Richard, and Gay Welch. *Unlocking the Secret Garden: A Study Guide.* New York: The Secret Garden Limited Partnership, n.d. Offers suggestions for preparing young audiences for the 1991 musical by Marsha Norman and Lucy Simon based on *The Secret Garden.*

Burnett, Constance Buel. *Happily Ever After: A Portrait of Frances Hodgson Burnett.* New York: Vanguard, 1969. Written for children by the wife of Burnett's son, Vivian; is based primarily on her husband's biography, *The Romantick Lady* and the author's own childhood memoir, *The One I Knew the Best of All.*

Burnett, Vivian. *The Romantick Lady (Frances Hodgson Burnett): The Life Story of an Imagination.* New York: Charles Scribner's Sons, 1927. Written shortly after Burnett's death by her son. Though largely laudatory, it is the only published source for some of Burnett's correspondence and other aspects of her life.

Carpenter, Angelica S., and Jean Shirley. *Frances Hodgson Burnett: Beyond the Secret Garden.* Minneapolis: Lerner, 1990. A short, generously illustrated biography for children.

Patterson, Myrna. *The Secret Garden: A Literature Guide.* Cambridge, Mass.: Book Wise, 1991. Offers suggestions for teaching *The Secret Garden* in the elementary classroom.

Thwaite, Ann. *Waiting for the Party: The Life of Frances Hodgson Burnett, 1849–1924.* New York: Charles Scribner's Sons, 1974. The most complete biography; a very readable presentation based on considerable research.

Articles and Chapters in Books

Adams, Gillian. "Secrets and Healing Magic in *The Secret Garden.*" In *Triumphs of the Spirit in Children's Literature,* edited by Francelia Butler and Richard Rotert, 42–54. Hamden, Conn.: Library Professional Publications, Shoe String Press, 1986. Discusses the role of secrets and their revelation in the healing process.

Almond, Barbara R., M.D. "*The Secret Garden:* A Therapeutic Metaphor." *Psychoanalytic Study of the Child* 45 (1990): 477–94. Describes the garden community as a "therapeutic milieu" that helps Mary and Colin "attain the skills and ego functions of normal latency and prepuberty" (487, 477); discusses the book's special appeal for prepubertal girl readers.

Barton, Ruth. "T. S. Eliot's Secret Garden." *Notes and Queries* 31 (1984): 512–14. Argues that Burnett's novel was a source for rose garden imagery in *Four Quartets* and *The Family Reunion;* compare with Heywood and White.

Bixler, Phyllis. "Gardens, Houses, and Nurturant Power in *The Secret Garden.*" In *Romanticism and Children's Literature in Nineteenth-Century England,* edited by James Holt McGavran, Jr., 208–24. Athens and London: University of Georgia Press, 1991. Compares gardens and houses as images of nurturance and power in *The Secret Garden, Great Expectations,* and *Jane Eyre;* describes Colin's dead mother as a moving force behind the healing magic in Burnett's book.

_____. "*The Secret Garden* 'Misread': The Broadway Musical as Creative Interpretation." *Children's Literature* 22 (1994): 101–23. Describes how the musical was developed and shows how some of its adaptations of the book are congruent with recent criticism, especially feminist criticism.

Evans, Gwyneth. "The Girl in the Garden: Variations on a Feminine Pastoral." *Children's Literature Association Quarterly* 19 (Spring 1994): 20–24. Describes how Rumer Godden's *An Episode of Sparrows* (1955) and Monica Hughes's *The Refuge* (1989) adapt Burnett's "feminine pastoral"—the portrayal of a "private and enclosed" garden that is "the image of the emotional life of the girl who tends it" (20).

Francis, Elizabeth. "Feminist Versions of Pastoral." *Children's Literature Association Quarterly* 7 (Winter 1982): 7–10. Relates *The Secret Garden* to recent feminist criticism, especially describing the garden as female space.

Gohlke, Madelon S. "Re-reading *The Secret Garden.*" *College English* 41 (April 1980): 894–902. An autobiographical account of the appeal the book, especially its treatment of illness and death, had on Gohlke as a child.

Griswold, Jerry. "Positive Thinking: *The Secret Garden.*" In *Audacious Kids: Coming of Age in America's Classic Children's Books,* 200–14. New York: Oxford University Press, 1992. Describes Colin's conflicts as Oedipal; discusses how the book is congruent with Christian Science doctrine.

Gunther, Adrian. "*The Secret Garden* Revisited." *Children's Literature in Education* 25 (September 1994): 159–68. Argues that the garden's "female energy"—expressed through Mary, Mother Sowerby, and Colin's dead mother—"is at all times predominant" and, thus, that "in the real terms of the text," Colin "never at any point displaces Mary" (167–68).

Heywood, Christopher. "Frances Hodgson Burnett's *The Secret Garden:* A

Possible Source for T. S. Eliot's 'Rose Garden.'" *Yearbook of English Studies* 7 (1977): 166–71. Focuses primarily on *Burnt Norton* but discusses also *The Family Reunion, The Confidential Clerk,* and *Marina;* compare with Barton and White.

Keyser, Elizabeth Lennox. " 'Quite Contrary': Frances Hodgson Burnett's *The Secret Garden." Children's Literature* 11 (1983): 1–13. Argues that the first part of the book, portraying a self-assertive Mary, is far more interesting than the second part, in which a domineering Colin pushes Mary to the periphery of attention.

Knoepflmacher, U. C. "Little Girls without Their Curls: Female Aggression in Victorian Children's Literature." *Children's Literature* 11 (1983): 14–31. Emphasizes the role of Mary's assertiveness in her survival; argues that the fantasy mode of Burnett's earlier "Behind the White Brick" allowed freer play to the female aggressive impulses ultimately domesticated in the realist *Secret Garden.*

Koppes, Phyllis Bixler. "Tradition and the Individual Talent of Frances Hodgson Burnett: A Generic Analysis of *Little Lord Fauntleroy, A Little Princess,* and *The Secret Garden." Children's Literature* 7 (1978): 191–207. Discusses Burnett's use of the exemplum, fairy tale (especially the Cinderella tale), Romantic concept of the child, and pastoral tradition in *The Secret Garden.*

Laski, Marghanita. *Mrs. Ewing, Mrs. Molesworth, and Mrs. Hodgson Burnett.* New York: Oxford University Press, 1951. Describes *The Secret Garden* as "the most satisfying book I know," especially for "those introspective children at war with themselves and the world whom no other children's writer has ever helped and comforted" (88, 91).

Lundin, Anne. "Secret Gardens: The Literature of Childhood." *Childhood Education* 67 (Summer 1991): 215–17. Uses Burnett's book as an image for the recollection of childhood reading one carries into adulthood.

Lurie, Alison. "Happy Endings: Frances Hodgson Burnett." In *Don't Tell the Grown-ups: Why Kids Love the Books They Do,* 136–43. New York: Avon, 1990. Describes *The Secret Garden* as innovative in its portrayal of "severely neurotic children" who are reformed primarily through their own efforts (142).

Marquis, Claudia. "The Power of Speech: Life in *The Secret Garden."* *AUMLA: Journal of the Australasian Universities Language and Literature Association* 68 (November 1987): 163–87. Uses psychoanalytic theories of Freud and Lacan to show how Burnett's book "images the power and the ideology of the late Victorian ruling class" (185). Focuses especially on the book's affirmation of patriarchal ideology as demonstrated by Mary's maturation into loss and Colin's maturation into gain in power.

Selected Bibliography

McGillis, Roderick. " 'Secrets' and 'Sequence' in Children's Stories." *Studies in the Literary Imagination* 18 (Fall 1985): 35–46. Identifies a variety of secrets or mysteries that may tease the playful reader of *The Secret Garden.*

Molson, Francis J. "Frances Hodgson Burnett (1848–1924). *American Literary Realism* 8 (Winter 1975): 35–41. Suggests some reasons for the decline in Burnett's critical reputation during her own lifetime and after.

Murray, Heather. "Frances Hodgson Burnett's *The Secret Garden:* The Organ(ic)ized World." In *Touchstones: Reflections on the Best in Children's Literature,* edited by Perry Nodelman, 30–43. West Lafayette, Ind.: Children's Literature Association, 1985. Discusses how *The Secret Garden* manages to "harmonize discordances," how the patriarchal, hierarchical social order emphasized in the second part of the novel is made to seem an outgrowth of the garden and thus "natural" (40).

Paul, Lissa. "Enigma Variations: What Feminist Theory Knows about Children's Literature." *Signal* 54 (September 1987): 186–201. Laments that Mary does most of the work of an archetypal identity quest while Colin gets most of the rewards, but argues that Burnett wrote the only kind of ending possible within the context of her world.

Phillips, Jerry. "The Mem Sahib, the Worthy, the Rajah, and His Minions: Some Reflections on the Class Politics of *The Secret Garden.*" *Lion and the Unicorn* 17 (December 1993): 168–94. Sees Mary's experience as typical of the alienation experienced by the colonial who returns home; explores the "ideological dissonance," as between spiritual equality and social inequality, in Burnett's text; citing Burnett's stereotypical portrayal of Yorkshire peasantry and education of Colin to be a responsible master, argues that "*The Secret Garden* rehabilitates empire by relocating it in rural England" (187, 193).

Plotz, Judith. "Secret Garden II, or *Lady Chatterley's Lover* as Palimpsest." *Children's Literature Association Quarterly* 19 (Spring 1994): 15–19. Discusses parallels between Burnett's and Lawrence's novels as well as the books' different attitudes toward maternity and class; speculates about why Lawrence might not have been willing to acknowledge a debt to a writer of "girls' books"; compare with Verduin.

Roxburgh, Stephen D. " 'Our First World': Form and Meaning in *The Secret Garden.*" *Children's Literature in Education* 10 (Fall 1979): 120–30. Explicates the novel according to Northrop Frye's theory of myths, emphasizing the role of the Edenic garden in Mary's and Colin's quests for identity.

Smedman, M. Sarah. "Springs of Hope: Recovery of Primordial Time in 'Mythic' Novels for Young Readers." *Children's Literature* 16 (1988):

91–107. Suggests that *The Secret Garden*, like ritual, allows its child protagonists and readers to experience sacred time and space in a way that provides a "natural, religious hope" (91).

Sullivan, Anita T. *"The Secret Garden." Kenyon Review* 11 (Spring 1989): 99–106. Describes how the author's recollection of her grandmother's garden was shaped by childhood readings of *The Secret Garden*, despite the fact that the actual and literary gardens were very different.

Threadgold, Rosemary. *"The Secret Garden:* An Appreciation of Frances Hodgson Burnett as a Novelist for Children." *Children's Literature in Education* 10 (Fall 1979): 113–19. Praises the book's characterization, style, and "moral"—"that self-reliance is a good thing in children and that listening to one's conscience may be wiser than listening to one's elders—advice that was heresy to many adults then and now" (114).

Verduin, Kathleen. *"Lady Chatterley* and *The Secret Garden:* Lawrence's Homage to Mrs. Hodgson Burnett." *D. H. Lawrence Review* 17 (Spring 1984): 61–66. Suggests that *The Secret Garden* might be an unacknowledged source of Lawrence's novel; notes parallel triads of landless female, disabled aristocratic male, and working-class male as well as similar use of nature to explore themes of rebirth; compare with Plotz.

Wallace, Doris B. "Secret Gardens and Other Symbols of Gender in Literature." *Metaphor and Symbolic Activity* 3 (1988):135–45. Discusses the secret garden as a metaphor for childhood memory and the female in a variety of authors, especially Dorothy Richardson's *Pilgrimage* (1912). Calls Burnett's book "the most famous secret garden in children's literature, or perhaps in Western European and North American Literature" (143).

White, Alison. "Tap-Roots into a Rose Garden." *Children's Literature* 1 (1972): 74–76. Cites parallels between *The Secret Garden* and T. S. Eliot's *Burnt Norton;* compare with Barton and Heywood.

Index

Adams, Gillian, 17, 47
Alcott, Louisa May, *Little Women*, 3, 10
Almond, Barbara, 19, 29, 30, 39–40
American Magazine, The, 13
Andersen, Hans Christian, "The Ugly Duckling," 88
animals and birds, 6–7, 26, 30, 31, 33, 35, 40, 42, 49, 52–58, 60, 67–68, 72–74, 76, 80, 89–91

Barrie, James, 14; *Peter Pan*, 4–5
Baum, L. Frank, *The Wizard of Oz*, 6
Bixler, Phyllis, 16, 17, 18, 20, 86
body, 32, 57, 86; appetite, 32, 55, 66, 76; senses, 55–58
Brontë, Charlotte 3, 17; *Jane Eyre*, 16, 93
Brontë, Emily, 3, 17; *Wuthering Heights*, 56
Brooke, L. Leslie, *Johnny Crow's Garden*, 7

Burnett, Constance Buel, *Happily Ever After*, 15, 89
Burnett, Frances Hodgson Burnett, "Behind the White Brick," 18; *Head of the House of Coombe, The*, 80; *Land of the Blue Flower, The*, 89; *Little Lord Fauntleroy*, 4, 5, 9, 10, 11, 14, 16, 35, 67, 71; *Little Princess, A*, 5, 10, 14, 16, 35, 67, 89; *Lost Prince, The*, 7, 80; *One I Knew the Best of All, The*, 6, 15, 89; *Robin*, 80; "Sara Crewe," 5
Burnett, Vivian, *The Romantic Lady*, 15
Burton, Virginia, *The Little House*, 88

Cameron, Eleanor, *The Green and Burning Tree*, 14
Carpenter, Angelica S., and Jean Shirley, *Frances Hodgson Burnett*, 89

Carpenter, Humphrey, *Secret Gardens,* 20
Carroll, Lewis, 14, 17; *Alice in Wonderland,* 3
Children's Literature, 16, 18
Christian Science, 32, 44–45, 73
class, 7, 17, 19–20, 27, 30, 39, 46–47, 49, 56–57, 64, 71, 75–83, 91–92
Cole, Joanna, *Best-Loved Folktales of the World,* 88
control, 27–28, 46–48, 49–51, 58–59, 80
Cooney, Barbara, *Demeter and Persephone* (illustrator), 88; *Miss Rumphius,* 89

death, 17, 19, 29, 31, 32, 34, 41, 44, 45–47, 48, 50–51, 63, 65, 67, 70, 90–91
dialect, 30, 39, 59, 78–79, 87, 92
Dickens, Charles, 3
didacticism, 7, 73–74

Eddy, Mary Baker, 44
Eden, 12, 17, 71, 71, 79, 85
Eliot, T. S., *Four Quartets,* 11, 16, 26
empire, 7, 20, 80–82, 91, 93
Ewing, Juliana, 14, 15
exemplum (moral tale), 7, 16, 70–74

film adaptations, 10, 34, 50, 55, 56, 91
Fleischman, Paul, *I Am Phoenix,* 89; *Joyful Noise,* 89
folk tales, 3, 16, 29, 35, 42, 57, 59, 88, 93; "Cinderella," 4, 5, 35, 67, 88, 89, 91; "Hansel and Gretel," 88; "How Sun, Moon, and Wind Went Out to Dinner," 88; "Little Red Riding Hood," 56; "The Sleeping Beauty," 35; "The Ugly Duckling," 88
food, 30, 32, 66, 71, 76, 77
Francis, Elizabeth, 17, 18, 85
Freud, Sigmund, 19, 45, 85
Friday, Nancy, *My Secret Garden,* 11
Frye, Northrop, 17

games, 6, 75, 81–83
garden, as book's center, 18; in Burnett's childhood, 6; and childhood, 11; and Colin, reflection of, 47–48; and Colin's mother, 34, 48, 53, 65–66, 69–70; and death, 34; Dickon's, 76; and female domesticity, 11; and female generativity, 69–70, 85; and independence, 28, 34, 48; and Mary, reflection of, 34, 38; as maternal space, 17, 53, 85; as nest, 52; as nurturant home, 52–53; and sexuality, 11, 19, 39–40, 54–55; symbolic meaning, 11, 70, 91
gender, 4, 5, 9–10, 11, 13–14, 16, 17, 18, 20, 39–40, 51, 83–86, 92–93
Gilbert, Sandra M., and Susan Gubar, *The Madwoman in the Attic,* 17
Glavin, Helen, 10
Godey's Lady's Book, 4
Gohlke, Madelon, 17
Grahame, Kenneth, 6, 14; *Dream Days,* 4; *The Golden Age,* 4, 5, 6; *The Wind in the Willows,* 7, 41
Green, Roger Lancelyn, *Tellers of Tales,* 14–15, 17
Griffith, Judith Ann, *The Land of the Blue Flower,* 89
Griswold, Jerry, 10, 19, 33–34, 46
Gunther, Adrian, 18, 85–86

Index

Hamilton, Virginia, *The House of Dies Drear,* 90

Hawthorne, Nathaniel, *A Wonder Book,* 3

healing, 6, 13, 19, 43, 47, 51, 60, 66, 70

Hughes, Thomas, *Tom Brown's School Days,* 3

illness, 25, 44–46, 63–64, 70

Inglis, Fred, 17

India, 7, 25–26, 30, 33, 38, 46, 51, 57, 80–82, 88, 90, 91

isolation, 25–29, 34, 37, 70, 90

Ives, David, 10

Keyser, Elizabeth, 18, 28, 83

Kingsley, Charles, *Water Babies,* 3

Kipling, Rudyard, 14, 17; *The Jungle Book,* 7; *Kim,* 7

Knoepflmacher, U. C., 18, 28, 86

Lacan, Jacques, 19

language, 58–59

Laski, Marghanita, *Mrs. Ewing, Mrs. Molesworth and Mrs. Hodgson Burnett,* 14–15

Lawrence, D. H., *Lady Chatterley's Lover,* 11, 56–57

Little, Jean, *Little by Little,* 90

London, Jack, *The Call of the Wild,* 6

London *Times,* 9, 10

Lunn, Janet, *The Root Cellar,* 12

Lurie, Alison, 10, 19, 81

MacDonald, George, 14

McDermott, Gerald, *Daughter of Earth,* 89

McGillis, Roderick, 17

magic, 19, 35–36, 57–61, 63, 66, 67–69, 72, 83, 88, 89, 91

Marquis, Claudia, 19, 20, 80, 84, 85

Mayne, William, 17

"Mistress Mary, Quite Contrary," 25, 27, 38

Molesworth, Mary, 14, 15

Molson, Francis, 14, 16

Montgomery, L. M., 6; *Anne of Green Gables,* 5

Mott, Frank Luther, 12

Murray, Heather, 19–20, 80, 84

musical adaptation, 10, 18–19, 67, 91

myth, 7, 8, 17, 37, 41–42, 51, 72, 88–89, 91

narration, 73–74; narrator, 30–31, 35, 42, 44, 57, 64, 74, 79, 81

Nesbit, Edith, 14, 15; *The Story of the Treasure Seekers,* 6; *The Five Children and It,* 5

New York *Times,* 9

Norman, Marsha, 10, 18–19, 67, 91

O'Brien, Margaret, 10

opera adaptation, 10

orphans, 5, 16, 34, 70

Pan, 7, 41–42, 71

parental nurturance, 26, 28, 44, 51, 53–54, 58, 63–70, 83, 85

pastoral, 6, 17, 18, 21, 71–72

Paterson, Katherine, *Bridge to Terabithia,* 12, 89

patriarchal authority, 40–41

Paul, Lissa, 18, 83

Pearce, Philippa, *Tom's Midnight Garden,* 12, 17

Phillips, Jerry, 20, 80, 86

Plishka, Greg, 10

Plotz, Judith, 40, 56–57

Poe, Edgar Allan, "The Fall of the House of Usher," 33

Potter, Beatrix, *Peter Rabbit,* 6–7

Proddow, Penelope, *Demeter and Persephone,* 88

psychological interpretation, 19, 29–34, 39–40, 45–46, 49, 63–67

race, 30, 92
Ransome, Arthur, 17
readership, 8, 9–10, 11–12, 13, 15, 74, 86, 87, 93
realism, 4, 35, 42, 93
religion, 32, 59–61, 70–73
repetition, 25, 61,62, 70; parallelism, 34, 37–38, 41, 43–44, 54, 62, 69–70; recapitulation, 47–49, 61–62; reenactment, 49, 59–60, 70
Ringgold, Faith, *Tar Beach*, 89
ritual, 17, 59–61, 70, 72
Roberts, Charles G. D., 6
romance, 3–4, 35
Romance of the Rose, 54
Romanticism, 3, 6–7, 17, 93
Rousseau, Jean–Jacques, *New Eloise*, 11, 54; *Emile*, 11
Roxburgh, 17

St. Nicholas Magazine, 5
seasonal cycle, 41, 51, 55, 57, 68, 70, 88, 90
secrecy, 5–6, 17, 34, 35–36, 41, 42, 43, 47–48, 49, 54, 80–81, 87, 90
self-assertion, 40–41
serialization, 13, 41
Seton, Ernest Thompson, 6
Sewell, Anna, *Black Beauty*, 6
sexuality, 11, 19, 39–41, 54–57
Sheppard, Nona, 10
Simon, Lucy, 10, 91
Smedman, M. Sarah, 17, 20
Smith, Lillian, *The Unreluctant Years*, 14

Spenser, Edmund, *The Faerie Queene*, 71
Sprenak, Charlene, *Lost Goddesses of Early Greece*, 88
Steig, William, *Sylvester and the Magic Pebble*, 88
Stevenson, Robert Louis, 14; *Kidnapped*, 4; *Treasure Island*, 4
structure, 62
Sullivan, Anita T., 11
symbolism, 13, 26, 37, 91

Thackeray, William Makepeace, *The Rose and the Ring*, 3
Theocritus, 71
Threadgold, Rosemary, 17, 81
Thwaite, Ann, *Waiting for the Party*, 15–16, 18, 29
Townsend, John Rowe, *Written for Children*, 15, 17
transformations, 17, 36, 57–60, 62, 66, 70, 74, 88; rebirths, 7, 51, 69–71
Twain, Mark, 6; *Huckleberry Finn*, 4, 16; *Tom Sawyer*, 4, 5,

Verduin, Kathleen, 56
Virgil, 71

Yonge, Charlotte, 14
Youth's Companion, 9–10

Wallace, Doris B., 11
White, Alison, 16
White, E. B., *Charlotte's Web*, 90
White, Robert Lee, 16
Wiggin, Kate Douglas, 6; *Rebecca of Sunnybrook Farm*, 5; *Mother Carey's Chickens*, 53
Wordsworth, William, *The Prelude*, 6

The Author

Phyllis Bixler is professor of English at Southwest Missouri State University, where she teaches literature for children and young adults. She has published a book and various articles on the life and works of Frances Hodgson Burnett. Two of these articles, "Tradition and the Individual Talent of Francis Hodgson Burnett: A Generic Analysis of *Little Lord Faunterloy*, *A Little Princess*, and *The Secret Garden*" (1978) and "*The Secret Garden* 'Misread': The Broadway Musical as Creative Interpretation" (1994), won the international Children's Literature Association award for the best critical article published that year.